To every Doxa Deo partner.
May you live in the fullness of this
revelation of the Good News.

Not Do But Done

Living from the completed work of Christ

By Alan Platt

Originally published as We Start at Finish: Living from the completed work of Christ by Faith Story Publishing in 2012, Tetelestai Media in 2014, Struik Christian Media in 2016.

Published in 2021 by Tetelestai Media, NPC
P.O. Box 2430,
Pretoria, 0043, South Africa
www.tetelestaimedia.com

ISBN 9780639906416

Not Do But Done

ALAN PLATT

CONTENTS

WORDS OF THANKS

There are innumerable wor ds of thanks that go out with this book. So many people, who were part of our lives at different times, gave significant input to the content of this book. At the end of the day, this work expresses a conviction that was formed over many years, by the input of many people. Thank you to each one of you.

To Leana, my wife – thank you for years of encouragement and support and sharing in the discovery of this Word. Thank you for sharing this life with me. You are an amazing woman and an incredible person to share life with!

To Duncan and Amy, my two incredible children. Thank you for showing so much understanding while I have been busy with the "big things" of the gospel. Thank you for celebrating with me the privilege of being able to touch and influence the lives of other people. You are both exceptional people in your own right and I believe God will touch the lives of many through you.

To the Doxa Deo leaders and family - my greatest privilege in life has been the opportunity to embark on this journey with this spiritual family for the past twenty years. I cannot imagine a more beautiful expression of Christ's church anywhere else on the planet. Thank you for your input into my life, for the opportunity to talk many of these convictions through with you, and for the privilege of sharing them with you from the pulpit.

To Isak Burger and everyone else who championed this book – thank you for believing in this work and for your words of endorsement that add so much weight to its impact.

To Tes, my faithful PA - Tes, you are a champion in His Kingdom. I don't know another person I respect more, and who has more commitment to the Kingdom than you. Thank you for eighteen years of walking this road together, but most of all for your huge part in being able to put this manuscript together. May eternity reward you!

Gerrit Heymans, my faithful armour-bearer in this project – thank you for your contribution to the success of this book.

To Louise Buys, thank you for putting all my technical convictions into a flowing, readable product.

Thank you too Ingrid Stegmann for your help in this regard.

To the team responsible for the English product, I thank you! Rick Moser you have been a star – thank you for your enormous contribution!

Alan Platt

WORDS FROM OTHERS

Alan Platt exemplifies the gift of leadership as powerfully as any leader in the church today. In his new book, Alan leads us to freedom by revealing that Christians start their walk with God at the finish line. Performance based, two-faced, ungraced Christianity is debilitating. Our assignment has never been about what we can do for God, but what God can do through us ... if we start at the finish.

Dr. Ed Delph - NATIONStrategy, Phoenix, AZ, USA

The content of the following pages contain simple truth, yet truth so profound it has the capacity to rock your world. You may have been a Christian all of your life, but Alan Platt's words are likely to strike a chord in you that will bring a new harmony to your spiritual walk and song.

"Not Do But Done" is a message of the victory God has already secured for His followers, and your Saviour's desire to showcase YOU as a trophy of His grace! I highly recommend this book to every believer and, after reading it, challenge each to pass it on to someone else who may not have any idea of the extent of God's love for them.

Keith Boyer - Lead Pastor, 3D Church, Denver, CO, USA

My friend Alan Platt is changing the country of South Africa! I know, I've seen it first-hand. In this book, Alan does something amazing that nobody does better – he describes the Good News of the gospel in a way that will make you crave it! He is intelligent, passionate and relevant to every believer. His book will encourage every kind of Christian, dedicated or discouraged, and cause them to fall in love with Christ all over again. If you've ever needed to understand the magnitude of the "Good News" available to you, then this book is for you!"

Rick Bezet - Senior Pastor, New Life Church of Arkansas, USA

Alan Platt and the Doxa Deo movement are known around the world for teaching, living, and modelling principles that bring transformation to every aspect of society. I saw this first-hand in South Africa, and it changed the way I do ministry. This book provides the foundational teaching that has resulted in the reformation of many lives and multiple cities. The Christian world desperately needs this man and his timeless message on the gospel of the grace of God.

Ron Lewis Sr. – Leader at Every Nation NY, & KPIC, Durham, NC, USA

I am so thankful for Alan's influence and friendship in my life. He is a deep well of wisdom and revelation from whom all of us can gain time after time. His understanding of the completed work of Christ will certainly strengthen and empower all of us to live as Jesus meant for us to live.

Pastor Brady Boyd - New Life Church, Colorado Springs, USA & Author of "Sons and Daughters"

I have known Alan Platt for more than 20 years as a man of integrity and authenticity. Apart from being a visionary leader gifted with faith for city transformation and releasing city-changers, he is an inspiring and gifted teacher of the Word of God. I highly recommend "We Start at Finish: Living from the completed work of Christ" as a must-read for anyone who is serious about embracing God's destiny of being Christ-like and living a victorious life in the here and now through 'the abundant provision of grace and the gift of righteousness'.

Don Price - Pastor, Doxa Deo London, UK

Alan Platt has one of the sharpest minds and probably the most generous heart I have ever come across in a leader. His love for the Word and the Ways of God has been a constant source of inspiration to me in the twenty years of life and ministry that we have shared thus far. As a leader, he has developed the uncanny ability to discern, with a single 'taste', the 'ingredients' that have brought about the situation before him. And as a leader, friend and pastor, he brings the most amazing wisdom to the table, providing clear guidance and strategic steps toward solutions that lead to growth and transformation. In an age where teachers and communicators abound, often contributing more confusion than clarity on the issue of Grace, Alan provides us with a landmark work that takes us to the heart of the Gospel of Jesus Christ ... and then provides a clear, strategic path to the kind of personal and community transformation that comes from embracing that heart. This is one book on grace you will want in your library.

Rick Moser - Associate Pastor (Worship & Arts / Training), Doxa Deo Brooklyn, Pretoria, ZA

Alan Platt's opening of God's word has not only expanded my understanding of the gospel, it has ignited my interest in personalizing all that is communicated as God's Good News for me. Discovering that I am not an after-thought in God's mind as far as the gospel is concerned changed how I view myself and placed me in a more intimate, open space of flourishing in the course of living. This book successfully communicates to non-believers, confused believers and true believers in a manner that will cause all to respond with love and gratefulness! This book is a must-read for all!

JK Lehoko - Campus Pastor, Doxa Deo Inner City Campus, Pretoria, ZA

I have known Alan Platt as a friend and co-worker in the city of Pretoria for many years. God has given him the unique ability to take a truth and earth it in such a practical, applicable way that it is easily understood. In reading the manuscript of this book, I was reminded of a song we used to sing: "We are complete in Him ... It's not by works of righteousness but by His grace alone". This book will encourage you to enjoy the complete and glorious life that the Good News offers to every person who is willing to receive it!

Nevil Norden - Senior Pastor at Lewende
Woord / Living Word, Pretoria, ZA

I commend Alan for articulating the impact of accepting Jesus Christ as Saviour in one's life. He has succeeded in making a clear distinction between salvation and religious practice. The gospel of Jesus is all-sufficient to take care of the sin question as well as its consequences, namely guilt and shame. New life in Christ should be a season of celebrating God's grace and goodness towards His creation. I fully endorse this book as a must-read for all born-again children of God who want to understand their new identity and position in Christ. Well done, Alan.

George Mahlobo - President AFM of South Africa

Much of Christian life today is expressed in a language that urges us to serve God with greater devotion. I am so encouraged that this book does not reflect that understanding. For a post-Christian society like Europe, the news of the completed work of the cross and a liberated life in Christ is truly good news! Alan Platt is a global leader, whose heart has been captured by this revelation and he masterfully celebrates that understanding in "We Start at Finish"... no longer self-performing, but participating in what Christ has done for us!

Alan leads a movement of socially-committed community leaders, whose faith enhances their intelligence and global perspective. The vision for a book about the identity of man, fully restored in Christ, is a natural extension of his commitment to see cities across the globe blessed and local communities transformed.

Ioannis Dekas — City Leader, Doxa Deo London, UK

Alan Platt's fresh approach to this centrality of grace and the life of believers portrays the finality of our position as believers. His thorough unpacking of Scriptural texts is a road map to the true freedom we have in Christ. Warning! Warning! Legalistic, judgmental and self- righteous individuals should not expect to be pleased with Alan's conclusion. However, if you're tired of trying to be good, worrying about eternity and earning your way to Christ's love, this book is liberating.

Rob Hoskins — President, OneHope Inc., Florida, USA

FOREWORD

I crossed paths with Alan Platt in 1982. It soon became apparent that he was not intended to be a traditional pastor. Here was a natural leader with an exceptional combination of talents, gifts and personality. He not only had the insight, wisdom and strategic leadership abilities of someone much older, but he possessed these to such an extent that, with ease and spontaneity he is recognised today as one of the most influential spiritual leaders in the church world in South Africa, and even internationally.

He is the father of the Doxa Deo Network – a church model experiencing unprecedented growth and influence in South Africa, as well as abroad.

It is not only his leadership ability that commands respect, but also his exceptional insight into Scripture and the remarkable ability to interpret and articulate essential Biblical truths in a highly comprehensive and effective manner.

This is why the publication of this book is such good news. While I am convinced that there will be many more bestsellers coming from the fruitfulness of his thoughts and heart, this book, "Not Do But Done", is an important and significant landmark.

Without a doubt, this book is going to have a profound effect on the average reader. While some may experience it as radical, this book breaks open the heart of the gospel. I found it refreshing to see that the focus was placed uncompromisingly on Jesus Christ once again. The gospel is nothing less, and also nothing more than Christ Himself.

From the days of the early church, some believers have struggled to understand and accept that Jesus Christ's substitutionary death was all-sufficient. Was it too good to be true, was it too easy or has the gospel not been understood correctly? In the first decades after Christ's ascension, this was apparently one of the biggest problems Paul had to deal with. It is remarkable how often he refers to this in his letters – especially in Romans and Galatians.

Throughout the Middle Ages, the emphasis on people's sacrifices and their own merits filled the ecclesiastical picture from A to Z. It took the significant breakthrough of Martin Luther and the Reformation to get people to get rid of these traditions passed on from their ancestors and to get back to the heart of the gospel – simple faith in Christ.

It is this core truth that Alan Platt exposes and emphasizes in such an exceptional and unique way. It sounds like something new, but is actually an age-old and wonderfully-liberating truth. I believe the most probable effect this book will have on its readers is this – that sincere and genuine believers and seekers will realize that Christ did enough, that He did everything and that we are able to live from the fullness of this complete work with grateful hearts.

What makes this book such an exceptional read is the contemporary idiom in which it is written. The consistent examples from our modern world show that it is not a dry, dogmatic document, but an easily- understandable and digestible explanation of the greatest Truth on earth – that Jesus Christ has made it possible for us to become part of the family of God ... and that this is not our own doing. This book should not leave anyone unchanged.

Isak Burger, President AFM of South Africa

INTRODUCTION

Did you play the game "Chutes and Ladders" as a child – a game that could frustrate the most unflappable of people? You did your best to climb a few ladders to get to the top as quickly as possible, only to land on a snake, being sent back down the board from whence you'd come. As a player, you resigned yourself to the disappointment that awaited your next move, after having just celebrated climbing up a winning ladder! Most of the time, you spent the whole game moving up and down until one of the other players finally reached "finish" on the board.

This game is an analogy of the experience many Christians have in their relationship with God. They view their own Christian life as an attempt to avoid spiritual snakes (sin) and to climb spiritual ladders (good works and dedication) in order to reach the finish line (heaven).

Life then becomes an experience of having to do my part and give my best to do everything right and to try not to sin so that I can qualify for heaven. I focus on arriving at the destination – the square on the board that says "Finish"; it becomes the focus of the whole game. Things usually run smoothly for a while and I may even get it right to climb a few spiritual ladders almost right to the top, but before I know it, a snake swallows me up and I end up right at the bottom of the proverbial playing board.

If this light-hearted comparison reflects something of your spiritual life, then this book is definitely for you. This book wants to guide you towards a discovery about the greatest message on earth. This message has the capacity to impact every person's life and to allow them to discover that God has freed them from a frustrating view of life.

Christianity is definitely not about playing spiritual Snakes and Ladders in the hope of making it to the top to reach the "finish" square. The reality you need to discover is that the starting point of our relationship with Him is actually the "finish" square – this is not our final destination! We start at "finish"!

The starting point: "It Is FINISHED"

Christ has reached the top of this Snakes and Ladders board on our behalf. Our spiritual life begins at FINISH. We start right at the top, at the perfection that Christ has already achieved!

This is the core of the gospel. If you do not begin from this perspective, your Christian life is going to be one long journey of constant frustration. God wants to make known His eternal, unconditional love to us from this starting point.

In Christ, you already live right at the top in the "finish" square and no snake should ever catch you off guard again! When Jesus cried out, "It is finished!", we were included in a reference that changed our entire existence. Your spiritual journey involves discovering your true iden-tity. This discovery begins when we discover ourselves in Christ, and His declaration, "It is finished". The game is over – we have won!

So many people continue to believe that we are responsible for our own salvation. However, Man – in his fallen state – is never going to get it right on his own. We need a Saviour!

When your walk with God is all about how you try to do everything right to gain His approval and reward, you are going to find yourself constantly struggling with three 'W's:

Firstly, you muster up all your *willpower* and decide to give your best and always try to do what is required. But before you know it, you do something that you shouldn't and it feels like one of the chutes have swallowed you up! You are so ashamed about your failure that you feel completely condemned. Didn't you promise yourself and God that you would never ever do that again? You soon come to the realisation that your willpower is not good enough and you completely give up.

Because of this, you begin to *waver* – you are precarious in your walk with God. The one moment you are well on your way and at the top of the ladder, the next moment you are right at the bottom and feel like you are far from God.

This results in the third "w": *worry*. You worry whether the Lord still loves you and doubt that He really cares about you. You start to feel unsure whether the Lord knows about your needs and whether He is going to help you or not because you feel so far from Him. You even begin to worry if you are going to "make it" one day. It is as though you despair of ever reaching the top level, let alone get to the finish square.

When you function in this way, you try so hard to please God and to experience His blessing, but it seems impossible to attain. So you start all over again by scraping the necessary willpower together to begin climbing the ladder of good works again.

Craziness

The Apostle Paul addresses this very issue – the Snakes and Ladders mentality – in most of his letters to the local churches of his time. He finds it hard to believe that Christians are trying to do something that Christ has already done for us, and challenges the church in Galatia about this. The Message translation says it well:

A re you going to continue this craziness? For only crazy people would think they could complete by their own efforts what was begun by God. If you weren't smart enough or strong enough to begin it, how do you suppose you could perfect it?

Galatians 3:3

Craziness! Christianity is not about performing in order to reach a final outcome. But the gospel is unfortunately sometimes presented as something we have to do in order to receive God's blessing.

God has already rewarded us. This reward has to do with the fact that we are in Christ: If you are in Christ, there is nothing in this world you still need to do in order to be rewarded!

It is clear in his letter that Paul has reached the point of despair with the people in Galatia – they are playing spiritual Snakes and Ladders and are trying everything in their power to earn God's favor and grace. This is, unfortunately, how many believers still live today!

Jesus did it on your behalf

When Jesus died on the cross, He said: "It is finished!"

Our healing and restoration is already guaranteed based on His finished work on the cross.

This book is not just another addition to the thousand others out there appealing to you to serve God with more dedication. It is, rather, the opposite. It is the invitation to join me in seeing how great the salvation is that Christ has already accomplished for us.

This book, therefore, is for everyone who wants to put an end to their "Snakes and Ladders" spiritual life, and who desires to live from the declaration Christ has already made over their lives: "It is finished!"

1

GOD'S GREAT MYSTERY

What is the first thing that comes to mind when someone tells you they have good news for you? Are you a little sceptical and expect it to be followed with a "but ..."? It's like the man who says to his friend, "I've got good news and bad news. The good news is that I bought you a ticket to the World Cup Final. The bad news is that you need to buy your own air ticket to get there." That's not entirely good news, is it?

Also, not everyone has the same definition of good news, because for some people good news always goes hand in hand with bad news. For example, if a teacher says to one of his students, "Johnny, you have not been selected for the team that will tour the Cape in July, but the good news is you'll be able to sleep late in your winter holiday," I don't think Johnny would think this was anything close to good news!

Good news must be good news – without buts, hidden agendas or deceptive fine print. There must be no trace of any bad news whatsoever – as was the case with the couple I heard about recently.

Both of them were already in their thirties when they got married and they wanted to start a family immediately. Unfortunately, after many years, she still could not fall pregnant and they decided to begin in vitro treatments as a last hope of having a baby. After two unsuccessful attempts, they were completely devastated but they decided to go ahead and try the procedure for the third and last time.

The blood tests came back – it was good news and the entire family was overjoyed! Everyone started placing bets on whether it was a girl or a boy and would come around to their house with clothes and gifts for the baby.

What the couple did not realise, was at that stage they had not yet heard the full extent of the good news. On their first visit to the gynaecologist the rest was revealed: the sonar showed two heartbeats and a few months later they were the proud parents of a healthy baby boy and girl!

In the same way, the gospel is good news in the purest sense – there are no buts" involved. The word "gospel" comes from the Greek word euangelion, meaning "God's good news."

What does the gospel mean to you?

It is interesting to hear people's varied responses to this question. Some are extremely vague and refer to forgiveness of sins or that God does not punish us for our sins. For others, the crux of the gospel is escaping hell and as a reward we get to go to heaven. Well, I trust that I've already got you thinking about the true meaning of the word!

What would you say God's good news really is?

The Good News is only good news if you can profit from it! Not everyone is excited about the gospel because some people feel judged by it. Instead of being happy, they feel guilty and ashamed.

Many people experience the church as a place where your guilt is exposed and where you need to feel ashamed of everything you've done wrong. It's a place where you always need to put your best foot forward and look as devout as possible. If that's the case, it doesn't sound like the gospel is good news at all!

Many people think the gospel is only intended for certain people: your race, language or church denomination can disqualify you from benefiting from it. But if certain people are excluded from the gospel, for whatever reason, it isn't really good news, is it? How can it possibly be good news if it doesn't benefit you?

Is it possible that the gospel's true message has been lost somewhere along the way? Is it possible that the church is no longer the bearer of Good News?

The essence of the gospel for many people is the forgiveness of sins and the fact that God no longer punishes us for our trespasses. Paul agrees that this is definitely part of the gospel, but there is so much more to it than this. Ephesians 1:7 states it so clearly: "In Him we have redemption through His blood, the forgiveness of sins, according to the riches of His grace ..." Yes, we are eternally grateful that God has forgiven us our sins in Christ! But we limit ourselves if we believe that's where it ends. Paul continues to motivate us to gain insight into the fullness of this gospel:

That the God of our Lord Jesus Christ, the Father of glory, may give to you the spirit of wisdom and revelation in the knowledge of Him, the eyes of your understanding being enlightened; that you may know what is the hope of His calling, what are the riches of the glory of His inheritance in the saints ...

Ephesians 1:17-18

This is the purpose of this book – for us to discover and truly understand exactly what the gospel is all about.

The Gospel revealed to you

There was once a man named Saul, a Jew and an advocate of the Pharisaic law. He was just a young boy when he was first introduced to the study of Mosaic Law. By discover and appreciate God's thirteen, he was a committed and gifted student of Gamaliel, one of the most highly respected Rabbis in the history of Judaism.

Judaism is primarily based on the law God gave to Moses. For a Jew, fulfilling this law is the greatest and most fundamentally important thing you can ever do.

Saul was there at the stoning of Stephen, the very first Christian martyr. Scripture tells us that Stephen was full of the Holy Spirit and power; he was also a leader in the New Testament church. What was Stephen's crime that warranted him being stoned to death? He told people that it was no longer necessary to try to uphold the law in order to be saved. He told people there was only one way to be saved and that was to believe in Jesus Christ. Steven preached the gospel!

For the Jew, including Saul, any preaching that exalted Jesus Christ above the Law of Moses was totally taboo. This is why they so passionately persecuted the early New Testament Church.

One day, Saul approached the high priest and asked that letters be sent out to all the synagogues in Damascus. These letters requested the help of all the synagogues to locate and capture anyone belonging to the New Testament church, and to bring them back to Jerusalem. But while Saul was on his way to Damascus to execute his persecution plan, he had a radical encounter.

As he journeyed he came near Damascus, and suddenly a light shone around him from heaven. Then he fell to the ground, and heard a voice saying to him, "Saul, Saul, why are you persecuting Me?"

*A*nd he said, "Who are You, Lord?"

Then the Lord said, "I am Jesus, whom you are persecuting.

Acts 9: 3-5

Saul, who later became known as the Apostle Paul, had an encounter with Jesus Christ that day and received the revelation of the gospel. This revelation awakened a hunger in him to know more about this good news. He discovered that God had intervened in in the fate of humanity and that he, Paul, was included in that. He realised that the inclusion of man in the life, death and resurrection of Christ, cancelled the consequence of the fall of man. For this reason he spent three years in the Arabian Desert where God revealed to him the full message of the gospel!

Paul speaks of this revelation in his letter to the church in Galatia when he tells them that this good news was not thought up by people. He assures them that he did not merely learn of it from a person, but that Jesus Christ revealed it to him in person (Galatians 1:11-12).

The gospel is something which is revealed to you by the Spirit of God. The one thing you need to understand about the gospel is that it's a secret; a kind of mystery that has been hidden in the heart of God for all the ages. It was a secret that no-one knew about.

This is why Paul says that if the rulers of the age knew about this secret, or even logically understood what it was all about, they would never have crucified Jesus. But they did not know it or understand it.

Paul says that this is a profound wisdom that God has kept secret through all the ages: God established it before the beginning of time in order that we might receive His glory. The rulers of the age have never comprehended it. Had they ever been aware of it, they would never have crucified the Lord of glory (1 Corinthians 2:7-8).

God prepared the message of the gospel in love for us. Throughout the ages, He has eagerly anticipated revealing this great secret to His people. This secret was something that would have a radical impact on man's existence; it would make it possible for man to be who God had created him to be. It would fulfil man's deepest longing! This is what Paul meant in 1 Corinthians 2:9 when he says that no eye has seen and no ear has heard and no heart has understood what God has prepared for those who love Him.

Paul is not speaking of something God intended for us in heaven, or in the hereafter. That which God prepared for us in love, is for now, while we live here on this earth. It is, however, a mystery. It is hidden from us and can only be revealed to us by the Spirit of God.

There are things that God wants to share with us that can only be revealed through His Spirit. All our intellectual diligence and theological research will mean nothing if we do not allow God to break open His mysteries and thoughts for us.

In Matthew 16, Jesus had an interesting conversation with his disciples about who He is. He asked, "Who do the people think I am?" "Well," they answered, "some say You are John the Baptist, others say Elijah or Jeremiah or one of the other prophets." Peter was the first to answer His next question, "And who do you say that I am?" He answered, "You are the Christ, the Son of the living God."

The way Jesus responded to Peter's answer was confirmation that the gospel message and Jesus Christ's identity was given to him through supernatural revelation: "Blessed are you, Simon, son of Jonah, for flesh and blood has not revealed this to you, but my Father who is in heaven."

Years later, Paul received the same supernatural revelation ... that Jesus Christ is the Son of God and that Jesus came to reveal God's original plan for mankind. This is what Paul believed, and he hoped that God would give each person in Ephesus a revelation of this mystery. Paul, therefore, prays that God would give each of them a spirit of wisdom and revelation in the knowledge of Him and that the eyes of their understanding would be opened so that they would know the hope of their calling and the riches of their glorious inheritance in the saints (Ephesians 1:17-18).

I am the lowest-ranked saint by far. My claim to fame emphasises the fact that grace is a gift and certainly not a reward for good behaviour. His grace alone qualifies me to declare this unexplored treasure of Christ in the nations.

> *The unveiling of this eternal secret is to bring into public view an association that has always been hidden in God; Jesus Christ is the blueprint of creation.*
>
> *Ephesians 3:8-9, THE MIRROR*

My desire is that the Lord will open our eyes in this time so that we can also know His everlasting plan that He has had for us throughout the ages. God's intention is for all of us to receive this revelation through the working of His Spirit.

Jesus Christ is the key

When we receive insight, we understand exactly what this Good News involves. The key to unlocking this secret is found in the words of Peter, who said to Jesus, "You are the Christ, the Son of the living God."

The key to this mystery is believing that Jesus is the Son of God and that He came to carry out a complete work on the cross. He is the centre of the gospel. If He had not been willing to offer Himself as the ultimate sacrifice for each person, becoming sin for us and allowing us to share in His glory, there would be no good news for anyone. The key to the gospel is in Christ's obedience, not in ours!

... so also by one Man's obedience many will be made righteous.

Romans 5:19b

Paul tells the church in Corinth that he only wants to talk about one thing – Jesus Christ who was crucified for us. The key to understanding the mystery of the gospel is understanding who He is and how His death on the cross impacts us. Understanding this unlocks God's eternal plan for mankind.

From the beginning of creation, God has carried this plan for mankind in His heart, which has now been revealed through His Son. This revelation of God's plan has been the best news for every single person throughout the history of mankind!

Elements of the mystery are revealed to the prophets

Throughout the Old Testament we see constant references to this mystery of God's master plan!

Just after the fall, we discover our first clue – God clothed Adam and Eve with the skin of an animal after they realised that they were naked. The blood of an innocent animal was a reference to the blood of Christ and a symbol of the righteousness with which we would be clothed, in Christ.

Years later, God would ask Abraham to sacrifice his long-awaited, only son. The moment Abraham took the knife in order to kill Isaac, God stopped him; when Abraham looked up, he saw a ram caught in the thicket behind him; he took the ram and sacrificed it as a burnt offering in place of his son; God provided a ram to sacrifice in place of Isaac. Once again, the blood of an innocent animal provides a clue or reference to Christ who would later die in our place.

Exodus 12 contains a similar clue: The Israelites slaughtered a Passover lamb on the night before they would be freed from slavery; the blood of the innocent lamb smeared on the doorframe was the sign to the angel of death to pass over their house and not take the life of the firstborn child. Again we see how an innocent lamb died as a substitute – just like the innocent, spotless Lamb of God would later die in our place.

God also shared elements of this mystery personally to people who sincerely sought after Him and served Him. They were then able to long for the day when the Messiah would come and they passionately prophesied about everything that would take place. The Psalmist sings of this prophetically when he declares how God has done marvellous things through showing His saving power and revealing His righteousness in the sight of all the nations so that the ends of the earth will see His salvation (Psalm 98:1-3).

There are many passages in the Word predicting the coming of Jesus as Saviour and Mediator. For me, one of the most beautiful of these is found in the book of Isaiah, where he writes of the crucifixion:

Surely He has borne our grieves and carried our sorrows; Yet we esteemed Him stricken, Smitten by God, and afflicted.

But He was wounded for our transgressions, He was bruised for our iniquities;

The chastisement for our peace was upon Him, And by His stripes we are healed.

All we like sheep have gone astray;

We have turned, every one, to his own way;

And the Lord has laid on Him the iniquity of us all. He was oppressed and He was afflicted,

Yet He opened not His mouth;

He was led as a lamb to the slaughter,

And as a sheep before its shearers is silent, So He opened not His mouth.

He was taken from prison and from judgment, And who will declare His generation?

For He was cut off from the land of the living;

For the transgressions of My people He was stricken. And they made His grave with the wicked —

But with the rich at His death, Because He had done no violence, Nor was any deceit in His mouth.

Isaiah 53: 4-11, NKJV

When we hear Isaiah prophesy like this, we know it is not merely a clue or some kind of reference. In this instance we see a man speaking accurately and insightfully of things that would happen way beyond his lifetime. He had a revelation of what was to come – a revelation of the gospel and the implications this gospel would have.

Isaiah continues to prophesy about the implications of Christ's crucifixion for mankind in Chapter 61:

"*The Spirit of the Lord God is upon Me, Because the Lord has anointed Me*

To preach good tidings to the poor;

He has sent Me to heal the broken-hearted, To proclaim liberty to the captives,

And the opening of the prison to those who are bound; To proclaim the acceptable year of the Lord,

And the day of vengeance of our God; To comfort all who mourn,

To console those who mourn in Zion, To give them beauty for ashes,

The oil of joy for mourning,

The garment of praise for the spirit of heaviness; That they may be called trees of righteousness, The planting of the Lord, that He may be glorified."

Isaiah 61:1-3

Isaiah must have looked forward to this day with so much expectation and longing, and written down this prophecy with such urgency in his heart.

It would be almost 700 years later when Jesus would stand in the synagogue one day and quote this exact passage of scripture to the people. After He had read it and opened the scroll, the moment arrived where He said to them, "Today, this scripture is fulfilled in your hearing."

The time had come – it was no longer time for clues and references. The Messiah had finally come and the New Testament, proclaiming how we are saved by grace, was finally set in motion.

On the cross when Jesus said, "it is finished," He was declaring that He had fulfilled every single requirement. That which had been predicted and anticipated for so long had finally come to pass. God kept His Word and reconciled humanity to Himself!

The New Testament presents the full picture

The Old Testament is packed with clues about the Messiah who was yet to come. The prophets prophesied concerning the grace which was destined for us.

These clues and prophecies are very much like a wife who bought her husband a drill for his birthday. She actually bought the drill well before his birthday, and from the time she bought it, right up to his birthday, she kept hearing him say, "If only I had a drill." She knew he actually already had a drill, but she couldn't tell him because the time had not yet come – his birthday was still to come. So she tried to encourage him: "Darling, you never know. Maybe you'll get a drill one day?" She knew the drill had already been paid for and that he would definitely receive it on his birthday. She just needed to encourage him to keep believing and living with expectation.

The Old Testament prophets knew about this grace we would receive – but the time was not yet right. Today, however, it is a completely different story because the time has already come. This mystery has already been revealed!

This is why Paul writes in Romans 16:25 that his task was to announce the good news of Jesus Christ and also the mystery that God had hidden from the very beginning. This plan had remained a mystery throughout the ages, but had now been revealed. It was being made known to the people so they could believe and embrace this good news. The impact of this good news is so significant that the whole of creation was waiting for it and even the angels were watching for it to be revealed:

... things which angels desire to look into.

1 Peter 1:12

For the earnest expectation of the creation eagerly waits for the revealing of the sons of God.

Romans 8:19

Can it be that the angels, who know what the gospel really entails, cannot wait for the realisation of this salvation plan? To the heavenly beings, we are the showground of God's grace!

Our salvation can never be underestimated! It is proof of Christ's power! Those who are saved are God's trophy!

Man's response

I wonder if we have ever realised how good the Good News is and discovered the implications this Good News has in our lives? I am convinced that thousands of Christians go through life without fully realising this glorious inheritance God meant for us.

Many are still where Paul was before he had an encounter with Jesus – they still place the full responsibility for their salvation on themselves. Basically, they try upholding the law by doing good works; hoping to win God's approval.

Meanwhile, God has already placed all the responsibility on Himself. There is nothing more you need to do to validate your salvation. Jesus Christ has completely disqualified us from all guilt and qualified us all for a life of victory and abundance!

Others are under the impression that they just need to wait patiently until they manage to convince God to give us this glory. But we are the ones who actually need to discover this glory that was made available to us through Christ. God revealed His plan for mankind through the cross of Christ. The engineer of the universe worked out our salvation down to the finest detail!

This grace shown towards us communicates a wisdom and discernment of our worth that completely surpasses any defini-

tion. The secret is out! His cherished love-dream now unfolds in front of our very eyes

Let me use the analogy of a gift that has been wrapped beautifully in colourful paper and has your name written on it. This gift is something that has been specifically chosen for you by someone because it is something you have always wanted. All you need to do is open it and enjoy it. You don't have to do anything to earn it. You just need to be willing to open it, with gratitude in your heart, and when you make use of it, to really enjoy the value it brings to your life. The joy on your face is enough to satisfy the person who gave it to you.

It is the same with the gospel! It is just like a gift we receive from the heart of God that radically changes our lives. At the same time, it brings Him so much joy because we are the trophy, the proof of His victory over His enemies!

In John 12 we read about a group of Greeks who went to a festival in order to meet Jesus. They went to Phillip and asked him to pass on the message of their desire to see this miracle-working Rabbi. Jesus knew that He represented God's intention for every human and answered them: "I tell you the truth, unless a grain of wheat falls to the ground and dies, it remains only a single seed; but if it dies, it produces much fruit."

Isaiah also said: "He will see his seed." Jesus was that grain of wheat that fell to the ground and died so that it would produce much fruit. Jesus was the seed; today we are the harvest. We are the reward of His suffering! He wants us to discover that all the properties that we admire in Him are also in us, because we are the harvest coming from that grain of wheat.

Paul's entire life's purpose on this earth was to get people to grasp this truth. He wanted every person to share in this great mystery of God.

The unveiling of this eternal secret is to bring into public view an association that has always been hidden in God; Jesus Christ is the blueprint of creation.

Ephesians 3:9, THE MIRROR

May we all discover and appreciate God's great wisdom, revealed to us in the gospel! May this good news captivate your heart to such an extent that you will also dedicate your life to sharing this message with others!

2

MY GOSPEL

Have you ever arranged a surprise party for someone or even just been on the receiving end of one? Women are particularly good at organising kitchen teas or baby showers. It's always interesting to see how the people who attend these teas, or those who organise them, seem to enjoy them more than the people for whom they are arranged!

So much effort goes into arranging a surprise party. The person for whom it is being arranged is usually blissfully unaware of all the preparations being made for her big day – there are people buying her favorite food, looking for her favorite music and buying her special gifts.

There is a real buzz when the guests arrive and everyone wants to know what the plan of action was to get the guest of honour there without her knowing anything. When the guest of honour arrives, everyone remains as calm as possible and waits for her response … how will she react when she finds out? The guest of honour is usually ecstatic when she realises that someone has gone to all the trouble and expense of organising a party that she did not necessarily ask for, expect or deserve!

Just like this surprise party, God, in His love and grace, planned something for us – He sent His Son to die on the cross for us so that we could live guilt-free. It is a gift we did not ask for, expect or deserve. God specially prepared this gift for us and so desires to reveal it and give it to us.

Can you imagine how disappointed God must be if, for whatever reason, someone does not want to receive it? This gospel is a gift which is meant for all of humanity – and that includes you and me!

My Gospel

The book of Romans lays a foundation for the Christian life and is considered to be one of Paul's greatest theological bequests. He begins Romans by introducing himself as a servant of Jesus Christ and as someone who is set apart to preach the gospel. He also makes it clear right from the beginning that he is not ashamed of the gospel, for it is the power of God to salvation for everyone who believes.

It is interesting that Paul speaks of the gospel a few times in the first chapter. He starts off by referring to the gospel of God and then he speaks of the gospel of Christ. At the end of Romans, after systematically laying the foundation for us and explaining the full meaning of the gospel, he refers to it as "my gospel":

Now to Him who is able to establish you according to my gospel and the preaching of Jesus Christ, according to the rev-

*elation of the mystery kept secret since the world began but now
made manifest ...*

Romans 16:25, 26

My gospel? There is a progression in Paul's experience
of the gospel. He knows that the gospel begins with the
Father and is revealed through Christ. Paul then eventually realises that God had included him in this gospel
long before he was born. Finally, the gospel becomes his
own personal story because he has been included in God's
great love story!

It is my good news!

This good news so overwhelmed Paul that he spent the rest
of his life telling others about it in order that they might
come to the realisation that they were included in it. As we
have already seen, good news is only good news if it really
is good news. Furthermore, good news is only really good
news for someone if it affects them directly.

How does it benefit me if my brother calls me and says,
"Good news! I won an overseas holiday and I fly out next
Monday."? This is fantastic news, but it is not necessarily
good news for me because it does not include me – it brings
no change in my own life. When he leaves on the aeroplane
on Monday, I still have to go to work. But if my brother
calls me and says, "Good news! I won an overseas holiday
and you're invited to come with me," it has a completely

different implication on my life! This time I'm included and have a direct part in the prize he won.

In his letter to the church in Ephesus, Paul writes that God's mysterious plan includes Gentiles as being co-heirs who are part of the same body and are equally included in His redemption plan – God included you and me in His plan!

One Man for one man

The day Adam sinned, sin and death entered the world. It was like a virus manifesting its symptoms in a body: after Adam, all people were born into sin, without choosing to do so. Paul says in Romans 5 that one man's crime resulted in all men being judged. Everyone who lived from Adam to Moses was automatically sinful, purely as a result of coming directly from Adam's bloodline.

It was only when God appointed Moses as the leader of Israel that the law was given, which brought a distinct differentiation between right and wrong. The law came to reveal man's sinful nature.

What was the purpose of the law?

- It was added as a result of our transgressions... Galatians 3:19a

- The law was our disciplinarian that pointed us to Christ... Galatians 3:24a

The law made man aware of his sinful nature and his deep need for a saviour who would be able to deliver him. The law led us to Christ!

The fall caused man to lead an unworthy existence. Our lifestyle was determined by the dominant influence of sin and darkness. We could not help ourselves, or free ourselves from this predicament:

O nce you were dead because of your disobedience and your many sins. You used to live in sin, just like the rest of the world, obeying the devil — the commander of the powers in the unseen world. He is the spirit at work in the hearts of those who refuse to obey God. All of us used to live that way, following the passionate desires and inclinations of our sinful nature. By our very nature we were subject to God's anger, just like everyone else.

Ephesians 2:1-3 NLT

Each one of us was a prisoner, held at ransom by this situation. You and I were born in sin as a result of one man's sin. We did not choose it and we did not ask for it — we were trapped in an abyss of a meaningless life of sin. We all faced the same dilemma — our lives were swept along by sin's unseen influence.

*F*or as by one man's disobedience many were made sinners…

Romans 5:19a

We were under the power of darkness – a spiritual authority that held us hostage. This dictator exploited us and reproduced his character in us. We were all in this position – a prisoner of lust, perverted in our thoughts and behaviour; oftentimes driven by the madness of being addicted to sensory avarice and momentary pleasure, trapped in a meaningless existence.

When we read further in Ephesians 2, however, we are confronted with the good news! Man's critical condition could in no way quench the overwhelming love of God. He has always loved us relentlessly with an urgency and intensity and it is this love that saved us by grace:

*N*one of this could distract from the extravagant love of God, He continued to love us with the exact same intensity.

Ephesians 2:4, THE MIRROR

Just as the transgression of this one man, Adam, resulted in our judgment and death, in the same way, one Man's obedience brought us life and acquittal from this sentence. Just as one man was able to plunge all of mankind into sin, so this one Man, Jesus Christ, achieved freedom for all humanity:

*F*or as by one man's disobedience many were made sinners, so also by one Man's obedience many will be made righteous.

Romans 5:19

More than conquerors

Mamelodi Sundowns or *Orlando Pirates* are names that don't mean very much to the average Afrikaans-speaking South African. If you were a supporter of one of these teams in the soccer league, however, it would definitely be either good or bad news for you if they won or lost their games!

This principle of good or bad news is very clear to the majority of Blue Bulls, Lions, Cheetahs, Stormers or Sharks supporters in South Africa. If your team wins and someone asks you for the result, you are more than willing to say, "We won," without personally contributing anything to the victory! In fact, some supporters have never even set foot on a rugby field in their life and in some cases don't even understand all the rules of the game. And yet they feel that they are included in that moment of triumph – the victory achieved by their team becomes their victory. They celebrate it as though they won it themselves! Good news is, therefore, only of value to you if it includes you.

Christ obtained a victory that includes the whole of mankind. Christ's victory includes each of us personally, and this is what we need to discover. In Romans 8, Paul asks rhetorically if there is anything or anyone that could separate us from the love of Christ. He goes on to say that it is clear that despite us being believers, we are not exempt from things like persecution, hunger and danger.

The question is, "In the midst of all these things, is there anything that can separate us from the love of God?" The answer he gives us is a very definite 'no'; there is nothing that can separate us from God's love! Paul leaves the best part of his answer for last when he says that we are more than conquerors through Him who loves us!

Christ won the victory! He even conquered death! This is precisely where the good news becomes good news for you and me, because Christ included us and made us part of this victory. His victory is, therefore, my victory. His triumph is my triumph. It is no longer merely the gospel, but it is my gospel. The reality of the victory Christ won for us is activated in our lives when we believe it. It is almost like someone sending you a parcel in the mail. It already belongs to you one hundred percent – you simply need to go and collect it from the post office. We receive the victory that Christ won for us on the cross through our faith:

*B*ut as many as received Him, to them He gave the right to become children of God, to those who believe in His name.

John 1:12

As children of God, we now share in His complete victory. We share in absolutely everything He went through. Just as much as we share in His death, we also share in His resurrection. God came and revealed His love for humanity by sending His Son to rescue us from our fallen state. The Good News tells us how God succeeded in delivering us from sin and death. One moment, mankind was still stone-dead in sin, but the moment Jesus was raised from death, all of humanity was raised from death with Him! Each one of us just needs to believe it in order to experience it. Sin was previously the proof that we were spiritually dead, because sin controlled our lives. But through grace something happened to us – a transformation took place. There is only one scripture in the Old Testament that directly refers to Christ's resurrection and includes man in it:

Come, and let us return to the Lord; For He has torn, but He will heal us; He has stricken, but He will bind us up. After two days

He will revive us; On the third day He will raise us up, That we may live in His sight.

Hosea 6:1-2

Obedience through faith

Faith is not a passive confession but a conviction of the heart that leads to action. James did not say faith without works is dead for no reason. Faith without the actions that flow from it is, in essence, not faith. Even Paul made it clear that faith and works or obedience go hand in hand:

*N*ow to him who is able to establish you in accordance with my gospel, the message I proclaim about Jesus Christ, in keeping with the revelation of the mystery hidden for long ages past, but now revealed and made known through the prophetic writings by the command of the eternal God, so that all the Gentiles might come to faith and obedience...

Romans 16:25-26, TNIV

THE MIRROR says the following:

*B*ecause of what I am blessed to see in this gospel I am confident in God's ability to make you stand strong and immovable. I proclaim Jesus Christ according to the revelation of the mystery which was concealed in silence in the sequence of timeless ages, (this gospel breaks the silence of the ages, and reveals how God succeeded to redeem his image and likeness in man) but now is made publicly known; mirrored in prophetic scripture, the God of the ages has issued his mandate to make the mystery known in such a way that all the nations of the earth will discover the lifestyle (obedience) that the hearing of faith ignites.

Romans 16:25-26

The obedience that the hearing of faith ignites

The law and the Old Testament appealed to man's willpower to fully obey God's law. The New Testament is a realisation by faith of a new way of living life that completely satisfies a human being and brings glory to God. Living by faith supposes that I have a relationship with God, the fruit of which is obedience.

Imagine a man who says to a woman, "I love you and I want to spend the rest of my life with you and care for you. Will you marry me?" What the man is actually asking is, "Will you trust me? Will you believe me?" The proposal is a significant event in every woman's life because it carries with it huge implications.

If she accepts the marriage proposal, her subsequent actions are evidence of her faith. Her love and trust in her future husband cause her to do certain things and put certain things in motion. She immediately begins getting her wedding plans in order. She will pack up all her belongings and move into the same house as her husband after the wedding.

She does not do so against her will or to win his love – she has already won his love. She does what she does because she loves him and also wants to share her life with him. It is her natural response to his expressed love and the promises he has made to her.

My wife and I do certain things for each other because we love each other and not because we are trying to win each other's approval; we already have each other's love and approval. Our love for each other has certain consequences and the things we do for one another are motivated by love, not fear. I don't pick up the towel from the bathroom floor because I'm scared of my wife, but because I respect her.

My relationship with Christ works in the same way – I am not obedient to Him because I am working to be included in the Gospel or to win His favor. Christ has already paid the price. I am already included – I have already won His favor. I honour and obey Him because it is the natural outflow of my love for Him.

In the Old Testament, people's motive was fear – they were fearful of God because they were unable to fulfil the law. In the New Testament, our motive is love for God. When the eyes of my heart are opened and I understand the gospel, my heart is filled with love for God the Father and for Jesus Christ my redeemer. Paul calls this the obedience of faith – a spontaneous reaction to do what He wants me to do. This is the essence of the Good News!

God's purpose with the gospel

God's desire for man is no longer a mystery. He wants to share this secret that He had kept to Himself for years with everyone! The gospel is the declaration of this mystery, of good news for you and me! God's plan with the gospel was never to cause anyone to feel guilty about their sin or godless living. It was never intended to fill people with fear or judgment, as we have heard so often in Christian circles, consciously or not.

Paul says in Romans 2:4 (New King James Version) that God is rich in goodness, forbearance and longsuffering. Doesn't this tell you something? Don't you realise that God wants to lead you to repentance by His goodness?

God is good and wants to use His goodness to draw you closer to Himself. The good news of the gospel is that Jesus Christ paid with His life so that each one of us could experience the presence of God any time and also experience His love, goodness and favor in our lives. The good news is that everyone who was in debt has now been pronounced debt-free. Our debt is not only written off, but we can now receive God's favor without having to earn it:

Paul refers to this in Romans 5: 8-11:

*B*ut God demonstrates His own love toward us, in that while we were still sinners, Christ died for us. Much more then, having now been justified by His blood, we shall be saved from wrath through Him. For if when we were enemies we were reconciled to God through the death of His Son, much more, having been reconciled, we shall be saved by His life. And not only that, but we also rejoice in God through our Lord Jesus Christ, through whom we have now received the reconciliation.

The starting point

The starting point of the Gospel is, therefore, clear. One man's unrighteous act immersed mankind into slavery and, equally, one man's righteous act could free the whole of mankind:

*F*or if by the one man's offense death reigned through the one, much more those who receive abundance of grace and of the gift of righteousness will reign in life through the One, Jesus Christ.

Romans 5:17

God desires now that we would know the mystery that He had kept hidden throughout the ages. God sent Christ to make this mystery a reality for us. The mystery is that there is a new life for us, characterised by the favor of God. This new life makes it possible for us to be free from everything that held us captive as a result of Adam's transgression.

In this new life, we share in His death, resurrection and ascension. Because He suffered and died on the cross, we are no longer fallen people but are once again welcome in God's throne room; we once again have the same position of authority we had before the fall and even more. We are seated with Him in heavenly places where we rule and reign with Christ!

Paul says in his letter to the Ephesians that God, who is rich in mercy, raised us up with Christ because of His love. We are saved by grace and raised up with Him, seated together with Christ Jesus in heavenly places so that now, and in the ages to come, He might show us the exceeding riches of His grace and kindness (see Ephesians 2:6-9).

'Heavenly places' is no longer our destination, but rather our starting point! God sent Christ to give us the riches of

His favor. The gospel declares the fact that man is included in the favor of God. Through faith, the reality of Christ's death and resurrection becomes a reality for me too.

We, therefore, do not work to be good enough to reign with Him in heavenly places one day. No, Christ paid the full price – there is nothing more that we can do. We now respond to what He has done by believing it, and this faith influences how we then live.

3

AWAY WITH GUILT AND SHAME!

One day, a friend told me about her grandfather who had the custom of reading the Bible in his home every evening after dinner. The grandchildren each took turns to fetch the Bible, while Grandpa wiped the last few grains of rice or breadcrumbs off the table to make sure it would not get soiled when placed before him.

After reading a passage for the evening he would pray, always ending with the following words: "Forgive us all our sins, for Christ's sake. Amen." These words always brought some measure of relief to everyone sitting around the table, because for a moment it felt like they were once again blameless before God and for that short moment didn't have to strain under the guilty weight of sin.

As one of the grandchildren who would get a turn every now and then to fetch the Bible, this friend always wondered what would happen if she happened to die just before dinner, having to carry an entire day's worth of sin on her without hearing the words "forgive us all our sins," which could bring her relief.

It is perfectly normal to feel bad if you've done something wrong and feel good if you've done something right. We all have a conscience – the internal policeman that makes us feel uneasy and is quick to point out if we're on the wrong track. Paul says that even heathens, those who do not have the law as their guideline, do the things that the law demands. The way these people behave is proof that the demands of the law are written on their hearts. Their consciences also witness to this when they are caught up in an internal duel – being accused or excused by their own thoughts.

> ... for when Gentiles, who do not have the law, by nature do the things in the law, these, although not having the law, are a law to themselves, who show the work of the law written in their hearts, their conscience also bearing witness, and between themselves their thoughts accusing or else excusing them ...

> **Romans 2:14-15**

Our conscience is very sensitive when it comes to experiencing guilt and shame.

Guilt is like a weight resting on our shoulders after doing something we know is wrong. It is a bad feeling that does not want to go away. Guilt brings distance and a lack of confidence before God. Guilt always leads to judgment which in turn leads to fear, eventually causing a sense of distance and later even complete alienation.

Shame differs from guilt, in that it is an inherent conviction that you, as a person, are not good enough – it is self-judgment. Where guilt is the result of having done something wrong, shame does not need a deed to be done, but is a permanent sense of wrongness. Shame brings a humiliation that robs you of your self-worth. It leaves you with a feeling of inherent worthlessness and a sense of rejection. It leads to behaviour that reflects the conviction that you are fundamentally bad, deficient, sinful and unworthy. It is, therefore, a feeling of inferiority about who and what you are.

The effect of sin on Adam

Before the fall, Adam truly lived out the purpose for which God created him. He had an intimate friendship relationship with God and he ruled on earth. He lived out his intended purpose until the day he sinned.

Where Adam once enjoyed the freedom of walking with God in the cool of the night, he was now so full of guilt and shame that he hid away from God. He used fig leaves to cover himself, trying to get rid of his shame so he could freely walk with God in the garden like he did before.

But his own efforts to get rid of this guilt and shame were to no avail. Sin got its grip on him and the whole of mankind. He became a slave to sin and also lost God as his friend.

The Bible says that man died – this meant that he now strained under the weight of guilt and shame, that he lost the understanding of his authority and also no longer had bold access to the presence of God.

All have sinned and are in need of a saviour

As people, we are all used to guilt and shame. We inherited this from Adam and we cannot get rid of it. The result of Adam's one transgression was that everyone born after him was equally under the power of sin. Paul says in Romans 3:23 that all have sinned and fall short of the glory of God. This resulted in man becoming a guilt- laden being, held captive under the power of sin, causing him to drift even further from God. Man, in his shame, became a prisoner of a distorted identity and feeling of worthlessness.

Man was, therefore, guilty and felt ashamed. His identity was now that of a sinner and he lived and thought like a sinner. Paul makes it very clear that everyone is a sinner.

Paul makes sure that every person is aware of his sin and guilt, because only in so doing can he understand, appreciate and grab hold of the full implication of the gospel. When you go to the beach for a swim, there are usually life guards who keep a careful watch on the waves, the currents and the swimmers. The presence of a life guard is not very important for the person having a leisurely swim, awaiting the next wave to dive into. But the situation changes drastically when that person is suddenly swept away by a current and cannot keep his head above water any longer. He suddenly gains a much higher appreciation for the life guards, who have become his only hope.

If we do not truly realise how totally lost we were as a result of our sinful nature, we will never need a saviour and the saving work that Christ did on the cross for us will never be of value to us. Only when you realise the weight of your guilt and shame can you fully understand what Christ did on the cross for you. When you understand that you are completely lost as a result of your sinful nature Christ becomes your focus and your only hope!

Christ our Saviour

The good news is that all of us who were laden with guilt and shame have been set free by Jesus Christ! Just as the first Adam immersed us all into sin, Jesus Christ the second Adam delivered us all from it.

The principle is, therefore, that every man born from Adam's bloodline is born into sin. You and I, therefore, are also born sinners. Jesus Christ was born a man, just like you and me, but with one difference – He was born of a virgin.

Why do you think Jesus needed to be born of a virgin? Jesus could not be born from Adam's bloodline, otherwise He would also automatically have been born into sin. Jesus needed to be born of a virgin in order that he would originate from God's seed and not mans'. Mary's body served as the carrier of God's seed so that the Son of God could be born as a man without sin. He is Immanuel, God with us, God who became flesh.

This resulted in the fact that Jesus was the only man born without sin on earth and, therefore, could live without guilt and shame. For this reason, He was the only one who could qualify as the Saviour of mankind to rescue us out of sin. He alone could carry out the task of laying down his (sinless) life for (sinful) mankind. This is why Jesus says He is the way, the truth and the life and that no-one can come to the Father except through Him (see John 14:6).

Jesus had a choice ... He could have chosen not to die for us on the cross. But Jesus not being prepared to go through with the pain of the cross would have carried huge implications for us – we would never have been able to get rid of our status as sinners and would never have been reconciled to God.

Because He laid down His life for us, man can now live free from his state of guilt and shame.

The gift of righteousness

Man's sin had to be punished somehow. God did not overlook our sin or change His mind and decide not to punish sin. There was only one punishment for sin and that was death. Jesus was willing to carry that punishment on our behalf – He was punished for the things for which we should have been punished. God dealt with sin that came to destroy mankind once and for all when Jesus was crucified.

When Isaiah prophesied about the crucifixion, he said that it pleased God to strike Jesus. Why? Because He saw the salvation of mankind! Mankind was completely freed when Christ died and was raised from the dead. The crucifixion was a success – there is nothing else needed to save mankind; the price has been paid in full!

THE MIRROR puts it like this:

Scripture concludes that all men without exception are in the same predicament, they are imprisoned to sin; now faith brings the promise of immediate release within everyone's reach! Jesus Christ makes it possible for all to believe what God believes concerning their righteousness and restored innocence.

Galatians 3:22

We are, therefore, no longer sinners, but the righteousness of God!

Righteousness means that we have been declared "not guilty," or rather "innocent," by God and that we have been completely approved and accepted by Him.

The gift of righteousness means that we do not need to be punished for our sins. Why not? Because Jesus took the punishment for sin on our behalf and redefined our status from 'sinner' to 'righteous'.

This is why Romans 8:1 says: "There is therefore now no condemnation for those who are in Christ Jesus ..." The moment Jesus died, He took the sin of the whole world upon Himself. He not only carried our sin; but He became sin. An exchange took place – Jesus became sin and we were declared not guilty and became the righteousness of God.

*F*or *He made Him who knew no sin to be sin for us, that we might become the righteousness of God in Him.*

2 Corinthians 5:21

Righteousness is a position, an identity you receive based on your faith in the complete sacrifice of Christ. Righteousness is the position you hold in Christ. It is not something you receive in various measures.

You are either righteous or sinful – you are not one or the other at different times.

God loves you and delights in you
God's love for us moved Him to send Christ to earth to die for us on the cross.

John 3:16 begins with the words: "For God so loved the world ..." God's love for us was the complete driving force behind the redemption plan. The plan was not only to free us from sin, but it was primarily to restore our true identity, so that we could experience an intimate friendship relationship with God once again.

Your new identity

Before you met Jesus, you were known as a sinner. You had every reason to feel guilty and ashamed. But now your shame and guilt have been replaced with righteousness and confidence before God! You have received a new identity in Christ; you are innocent and completely accepted; you have been exonerated of all punishment!

The gospel (the good news) is about how God succeeded in ridding man of his old identity as sinner and giving him a new identity. Through our redemption in Christ, once again, we have become the image of God revealed.

There is more...

Paul says in Romans 5:17 that through the transgression of the one man (Adam) death reigned, but through the One, Jesus Christ, so much more was gained.

Through one man sin had a significantly powerful and negative impact on the whole of mankind, but Paul says that Jesus achieved so much more than simply neutralising or cancelling the effect of sin! In other words – Jesus did not simply even things up but He made sure that He added much more. Not only is Adam no longer the reference to my existence and identity, but Jesus Christ Himself has now become the reference to my existence.

Jesus Christ is our Saviour! Once again, there is so much more to the meaning of this word, salvation, than what we initially might think. 'Salvation' comes from the Greek word *soteria*, which also means wholeness, restoration and fullness.

Soteria not only refers to the forgiveness of sin, but also to the restoration of that which was lost or broken. Where man was broken as a result of sin, the gospel has the power to make us whole again. Salvation involves the total restoration of a broken person.

Let them rule as kings
God originally commanded man to rule:

> *Then God said, "Let Us make man in Our image, according to Our likeness; let them have dominion over the fish of the sea, over the birds of the air, and over the cattle, over all the earth and over every creeping thing that creeps on the earth."*
>
> **Genesis 1:26**

It was God's dream for us to live with Him in an intimate relationship and that we would reign as kings on the earth. Sin entered the world, accompanied by guilt and shame. These two forces caused us to become inferior beings and completely undermined our authority as rulers.

Guilt and shame oppressed all of mankind and made us slaves of an inferior way of living. There can be no greater news than to hear that we've all been totally freed from this lifestyle. The day dawned when our Saviour and

Redeemer died for us on the cross and delivered us from the paralysing effect of guilt and shame and restored and re-appointed us as rulers!

The gospel versus religion

It is essential that you, as one who has been redeemed, no longer fall into the trap of religion. To be religious, in the negative sense, is to do everything in your power to keep God happy and to try living up to His expectations in your own strength. Religion is man's attempt to rectify what Adam did wrong. Faith is understanding that nothing that we do right could ever restore our position with God – Christ has already done everything that was necessary.

People who cannot move beyond this point of view are called religious Christians – they understand that man once had a perfect relationship with God and that the fall resulted in separation between God and man. They also understand that Christ redeemed us from the power of sin and death, but it is as though the full implications of this truth have not yet sunk in.

Religious people try to live extremely carefully according to Biblical principles and by doing so they try to win and maintain God's favor. They see the Bible as a moral handbook, out of which we need to regulate our behaviour as fearfully and piously as possible. If we do not do so, or fail to get it right, we immediately become unsure of our position before God ... which influences our ability to come to God confidently and fearlessly. Asking God to forgive their sins at the end of each day becomes something religious people grab hold of in a desperate attempt to fulfil that which they could not achieve in their own human strength that day.

But we are in the privileged position of knowing that we are already forgiven. We can, therefore, thank Him for the complete work of salvation! We don't have to do anything else to be accepted or to earn God's favor.

When you, as a Christian, still feel you need to do things in order to win God's approval, you are no better off than any other person of another religion. The gospel is not about what you still need to do, but it is about discovering what Christ has already done for you.

Hebrews 10:14 tells us that it took one perfect sacrifice by one perfect person to perfect a lot of imperfect people:

It was a perfect sacrifice by a perfect person to perfect some very imperfect people. By that single offering, he did everything that needed to be done for everyone who takes part in the purifying process.

Hebrews 10:14, THE MESSAGE

Sometimes we, ourselves, cannot believe that Christ has already done everything for us because we are so conditioned to believing that we must this and we must that. Forget for a moment what you feel you must do as a believer, and reflect for a moment on the truth that you already have God's favor. Most people with a good religious background would probably experience tension at this idea. It almost sounds too good to be true!

Trying to contribute something towards your salvation is like doing what Adam and Eve did when they covered themselves with fig leaves to hide their shame. Paul stands amazed that there are Christians who miss God's salvation and continue in their own efforts in order to be saved:

> *Brethren, my heart's desire and prayer to God for Israel is that they may be saved. For I bear them witness that they have a zeal for God, but not according to knowledge. For they being ignorant of God's righteousness, and seeking to establish their own righteousness, have not submitted to the righteousness of God. For Christ is the end of the law for righteousness to everyone who believes.*
>
> **Romans 10:1-4**

The difference between religion and the good news of the gospel is that religion still attempts, straining under the weight of guilt and shame, to win the approval of God through its own efforts. For years, the emphasis of our religion has been man's sinful nature as a result of the fall. The focus of our message for years was the shame of the fall, which has overshadowed salvation in Christ. The good news of the gospel grew dim as a result of our sin-consciousness and our inability to live right.

God found us in Christ long before he lost us in Adam! Scripture tells us that God carefully planned our salvation in Christ before the foundation of the world. In Him, everything was accomplished to restore us to our original created purpose of being God's image bearers.

The good news of the gospel is that Christ carried the punishment of our sins for us and made us the righteousness of God! Instead of feeling inferior and useless, we can, therefore, enjoy an intimate relationship with God without blame!

If we preach anything else we are not preaching the gospel! Religion will get us nowhere. We cannot save ourselves and we can do nothing to win God's approval.

Man's response

The gospel is the good news that God is pleased with man – God is not angry or just putting up with man. Jesus came to earth to proclaim this mystery from the heart of the Father. God chose to devise a plan to make known His pleasure for man publically. The angels knew that a time of favor would come for man, which is why they expected man to be ecstatic to hear the news:

*T*hen the angel said to them, *"Do not be afraid, for behold, I bring you good tidings of great joy which will be to all people.*

Luke 2:10

"Glory to God in the highest, And on earth peace, goodwill to-ward men!"

Luke 2:14

The power of the gospel

No wonder Paul boasts of the power contained in the gospel:

*F*or I am not ashamed of the gospel of Christ, for it is the power of God to salvation for everyone who believes, for the Jew first and also for the Greek.

Romans 1:16

The power of the gospel is not only to pronounce us free from sin, but to place us in a position of total freedom, confidence and rulership. It is a power that makes people whole again. The power of the gospel, says Paul, lies in the revelation that we have now been declared the righteous-ness of God:

For in it the righteousness of God is revealed from faith to faith; as it is written, "The just shall live by faith."

Romans 1:17

Herein lies the secret of the power of the gospel; there is no good news in it until the righteousness of God is revealed!

Romans 1:17, THE MIRROR

Paul was completely convinced of the power contained in the gospel. He even says to the church in Corinth that he does not preach a gospel that he hopes will work – but a truth that stands firm, of which he is completely convinced.

He is also convinced that whatever happened to mankind as a result of the fall is something of the past, and that our salvation far supersedes it:

Therefore, as through one man's offense judgment came to all men, resulting in condemnation, even so through one Man's righteous act the free gift came to all men, resulting in justification of life.

Romans 5:18

The J.B. Phillips translation of Romans 5:18 reads as follows:

We see, then, that as one act of sin exposed the whole race of men to God's judgment and condemnation, so one act of perfect righteousness presents all men freely acquitted in the sight of God.

Paul places the fall of man and every single sin after that in comparison to the one act of Christ which freed us forever. The sacrifice of Christ far outweighs everything else. We are truly and eternally free from all guilt and shame!

The gospel is **good news**!

4

YOU'RE NO SINNER!

You know what metamorphosis means, don't you? You were taught the term in biology class. It is when a living organism adopts a completely new form and becomes a totally different being. The example we all know well is when a caterpillar turns into a butterfly...

We all know about silkworms – I'm sure all of us, at some stage or another, kept silkworms in an old shoebox and had to sell them or get rid of them when Mom got tired of having them around! Silkworms are strange things. They have fat little bodies and eat mulberry leaves all day and move around with cute little peristaltic movements. But the most important thing you need to know about a silkworm is that it acts like a caterpillar because it is, in essence, a caterpillar...

When they mature into adult silkworms they begin producing silk and shortly after that they spin themselves tightly into a bright yellow cocoon. Once the silkworm has been cocooned, it changes form and a completely different creature eventually emerges! A few days earlier it was still a silkworm and suddenly it has become a moth with wings!

The miracle of metamorphosis is that there is now absolutely no sign of the caterpillar ... the moth or butterfly looks completely different and you can hardly imagine that this beautiful winged creature was a fat caterpillar just a few days before.

Suddenly, he no longer moves with peristaltic movements along the ground, but has two beautiful wings with which to fly. He also no longer eats mulberry leaves, but lives off the sticky, sweet nectar of flowers and blossoms. The most important thing you need to know about a butterfly is that it acts like a butterfly because it is, in essence, a butterfly.

The identity and mentality of a sinner

All of us were just like the caterpillar ... as expressed clearly in these scriptures:

> 66*Behold, I was brought forth in iniquity, and in sin my mother conceived me."*
>
> *(see Psalm 51:5);*

> 66*... for all have sinned and fall short of the glory of God ..."*
>
> *(see Romans 3:23).*

We were all sinners as a result of Adam's one transgression, which is why we acted like sinners. We thought like sinners, behaved like sinners and spoke like sinners. This is why we walked around with this eternal feeling of guilt – guilt because we continued to sin, and shame because we were always convinced of our inferiority and that we were never good enough (not good enough for God, or for the people around us).

It is essential to realise that God never originally created man as a sinner, but Paul said that we all sinned and no longer partake in the glory of God.

When Paul refers to sin, he uses the Greek word *hamartia*. Sin does not merely speak of doing wrong things, because *hamartia* means to miss your purpose or target. It means that you miss the purpose for which God created you.

Whenever anything is used for something for which it was not specifically designed, it is bound to get damaged. All the qualities of that item function to ensure its effectivity.

For example, it is not recommended that you go out and hunt wild rabbits in your BMW Z4, despite it probably being a lot of fun to speed around off-road in a sports car. Unfortunately, the fun could never justify the damage that would be caused! The truth is, the car was designed for a completely different terrain and purpose. The principle is that anything that functions outside its created purpose will always get damaged. The reason we see so much damage in people's lives around us, is essentially that people are living outside of their created purpose.

What were you originally designed for?

This important principle can also apply to our lives. If you do not live according to the purpose for which you were created, you will also become damaged. This damage results in our experience of *guilt* and *shame* which leads to *pain*. Adam's fall caused these three negative effects. Because Adam lived like a sinner and, therefore, did things that were contrary to what he was originally created to do, the whole of mankind became damaged as a result. Before the fall, Adam was created and designed in such a way that he lived in total innocence before God, and he was able to rule and reign from this place of wholeness in his identity. After the fall he lost this privilege.

Unfortunately, many Christians think they are still sinners and, as a result, behave as though they are. Christ died on the cross to deal with your identity as a sinner – He came to deliver you by becoming sin so that you could become the righteousness of God!

One night, a Pharisee by the name of Nicodemus went to Jesus to find out more about Him. He knew that Jesus was a man of God and that He performed miracles because God was with Him. This is where Jesus gave the response about what it means to be born again: "Most assuredly, I say to you, unless one is born again, he cannot see the kingdom of God." (See John 3:3).

Of course what Jesus said did not make any sense to Nicodemus and he asks of Jesus, "... how can you be born again when you're already old? Surely you cannot enter your mother's womb for a second time to be born?" He must have wondered how on earth that could be possible? Knowing that Jesus was implying a new way of living, he wanted to understand how he would attain it. He probably expected Jesus to give him a list of laws he would have to live up to – laws that would require him to rely once again on his works and responsibility to make sure he did everything right in order to qualify or deserve to be born of God.

Perhaps he expected Jesus to give him the kind of answer that would help him, as caterpillar, to try to live like a butterfly every day so that he could earn God's approval and in this way qualify for God's kingdom. But caterpillars cannot fly! He was completely stunned with the answer Jesus gave him when He said:

*A*nd as Moses lifted up the serpent in the wilderness, even so must the Son of Man be lifted up, that whoever believes in Him should not perish but have eternal life.

John 3:14-15

As a student of the Law, Nicodemus remembered the story of the snake. We read about this in Numbers 21 where God allowed poisonous snakes to come into the camp and bite the Israelites. The people began to die and Moses begged God for help. God commanded him to mount a bronze snake on a pole that if anyone were bitten by a poisonous snake and looked up, in faith, at this bronze snake, they would be healed. This was a strange command, even for Moses, because a snake was the symbol of sin, unrighteousness and oppression and because copper (the primary ingredient of bronze), being a 'base' or impure metal, symbolised the sinful nature of man!

Jesus was now making these events applicable to Himself. He knew He would have to become sin on the cross in order to neutralise the poison of sin in man when sinful man believed in Him. But could Nicodemus fully understand this at that stage? Was it possible for him to simply believe in this Jesus in order to be born again, especially when He was comparing Himself to the snake on the pole?

There are so many people who have never had the opportunity to undergo this metamorphosis of being transformed from a sinner to someone righteous. As a result, they behave like sinners, because inherently they are still sinners. It doesn't matter how hard they try not to sin - a caterpillar can never be a butterfly, even on its best day...

The other side is even more tragic
There are others who have actually undergone this metamorphosis but have never realised its truth and effect. They have wings, yet they crawl around on the ground; they are righteous, but still see themselves as sinners. People think it is pious to say, "I'm just a sinner," and then to add, equally piously, "saved by grace". They continue to refer to themselves as sinners because they misunderstand and

underestimate the grace of God. If God has saved you from sin, delivered and freed you, how can you still be a sinner? This lie will continue to have a hold on you as long as you hold onto your identity as sinner, that is, as long as you believe you are a sinner, you will act like one.

Such people see themselves as caterpillars who have to try really hard to be a better caterpillar every day so that one day they might become a butterfly. The truth is, in Christ you have received the identity of a butterfly. You no longer have to crawl around on the ground. All you have to do is spread your wings and fly! A butterfly remains a butterfly even though it sometimes gets wet, dirty or hungry. As a born-again child of God, you are no longer a sinner who has to try not to sin anymore – you are righteous. Can you see how radically different this is from what most people believe? You have received a brand new identity – you are not a sinner anymore!

My new identity

After God delivered Israel from the destruction of slavery in Egypt, the Israelites could move to a new land, free from the Egyptians. They also had a new identity – they were no longer slaves, they were now God's chosen people. But the moment the slightest difficulty crossed their path, they were quick to yearn for their lives as slaves.

Sometimes we respond just like the Israelites of old: we are so well schooled in our old, sinful identity that we are, in some cases, prepared to fight religiously to hang onto it. Even though living as a sinner is destructive and holds absolutely no joy, the "I'm just a poor old sinner" identity is something so familiar that we want to hold onto it for all its worth.

But now that you're no longer a sinner, who are you really? Let me use the example of a second-hand car. The salesman will confidently say to you, "This car has been remodelled so beautifully, it's as good as new." While this may be true, the fact of the matter is the car is not new – someone has owned it and used it before you. The mileage has already clocked two hundred thousand and it remains a 2001 model. God does things differently, as evidenced in these Scriptures:

Therefore, if anyone is in Christ, he is a new creation; old things have passed away; behold, all things have become new.

2 Corinthians 5:17

Now whoever you thought you were before, in Christ you are a brand new person! The old ways of seeing yourself and everyone else are over. Look! The resurrection of Jesus has made everything new!

2 Corinthians 5:17, THE MIRROR

If we are in Christ, we are not simply a second-hand model that has been polished up. Rather, it's like we're a brand new model that has never been driven before, with zero mileage on the odometer! You're as new as someone who has just been born. No baby is born already carrying an old identity book, a criminal record or lengthy financial portfolio. You get a brand new birth certificate regardless of your family history! God does not make you as good as new, He makes you brand new! He allows you to be born again as someone completely different! If you are born of God as a brand new person, how on earth could you still be a sinner? You are also not a caterpillar that just got wings and a new diet – you are a butterfly to the very core!

2 Corinthians 5:21 says it like this in the New International Version:

> God made him who had no sin to be sin for us, so that in him we might become the righteousness of God.

If we have received a brand new identity in Christ, why then do we hold fast to our identity as sinners, when God has clothed us in a robe of righteousness? Righteousness is the greatest, deepest deliverance from guilt and shame. It is even more life-changing than stepping down off the stand in a court of law after the judge pronounces you not guilty. Righteousness is a position of total innocence. This righteousness is the foundation of your new identity and also the primary characteristic of who you are in Christ. God made Jesus, who knew no sin, to be sin on our behalf so that we could become the righteousness of God in Him!

Your identity has been exchanged

You were conceived and born in sin. You were once a sinner. Through the cross, however, a divine exchange took place between you and God. You exchanged your *guilt* for *grace*; you exchanged *shame* for *righteousness*; you exchanged past *hurts* for *wholeness*.

The old 'you' is dead ... stone-dead. You died with Christ on the cross. You were also pronounced dead and you were buried. But you were spiritually raised with Christ and are now a completely new creation! The old you died and the new you is now alive! You do not have a schizophrenic life of having two natures; 'the body of sin', the old nature, has been done away with.

Therefore we were buried with Him through baptism into death, that just as Christ was raised from the dead by the glory of the Father, even so we also should walk in newness of life. For if we have been united together in the likeness of His death, certainly we also shall be in the likeness of His resurrection, knowing this, that our old man was crucified with Him, that the body of sin might be done away with, that we should no longer be slaves of sin. For he who has died has been freed from sin.

Romans 6:4-7

You can't be righteous today and then if you do something wrong tomorrow not be righteous anymore. You don't lose your righteousness and then get it back if your behaviour says you've earned it. Your position in Christ is permanent. The moment your righteousness is dependent upon your works, you're busy with religion. Righteousness is a gift that cannot be earned. You don't have to fulfil a whole lot of rules and regulations in the hope of winning God's approval. In Christ, you are the righteousness of God.

Because you are now the righteousness of God, you can once again approach the Father with confidence. Jesus gave up this position so that our intimacy with the Father could be restored. He took the burden of sin upon Himself and cried out: "My God, My God, why have You forsaken Me?"

Take note that Jesus did not cry, "My Father", because at that moment there was no longer that level of intimacy between Him and the Father. The Father had to "forsake" Jesus because He had become sin in order that we could become the righteousness of God in Christ.

Discover the new you
Jesus Christ is now the reference point of your identity – He is the blueprint of your identity. Jesus is not only an example for us, but of us.

… because as He is, so are we in this world.

It was always the Father's intention that we live according to the blueprint of the Son.

He pre-designed and engineered us from the start to be jointly fashioned in the same mould and image of his son according to the exact blueprint of his thought. We see the original and intended pattern of our lives preserved in his Son. He is the firstborn from the same womb that reveals our genesis. He confirms that we are the invention of God.

Romans 8:29, THE MIRROR

Mankind is no longer prisoner to Adam's bloodline. We now qualify as a new race, a new species born of God:

For the love of Christ compels us, because we judge thus: that if One died for all, then all died...

2 Corinthians 5:14

The price has been paid once and for all. You do not originate from the sinful bloodline of Adam, but the bloodline of Christ. Jesus Christ is the definition of your true identity – your origin is now in Christ:

For whom He foreknew, He also predestined to be conformed to the image of His Son, that He might be the firstborn among many brethren.

Romans 8:29

The concept of "firstborn" comes from the Greek word *proto*. This word is not just numerical in nature, but indicates the nature or specification of something. In other words, we are designed to be able to live like Christ! If you hear this, it could sound conceited and vain. However, true humility before the Lord, and particularly in this context, is never to consider yourself a poor old sinner, but to be totally dependent on God and to recognise that there is nothing you can do to win God's approval. You understand that you needed a saviour to rescue you from sin and your own inability and to clothe you in righteousness.

Live from your new identity

The movie *The Princess Diaries* tells the story of a teenage girl living in New York who is struggling to find her place in society. Then comes a piece of completely unexpected news – she is actually the princess of a small European country and next in line to the throne. The film very humorously tells the story of how her grandmother tries to help her "unlearn" her old ways of doing things and teach her to act according to her new-found identity. This film made me think of the situation many of us find ourselves in. Each of us has received a brand new identity, but we often don't know how to get rid of our old identity as sinners so that we can rule and reign as kings.

The biggest problem is primarily in our thoughts. Just like the girl in the movie, it is sometimes difficult for us to think and behave differently. Paul says we shouldn't conform our behaviour to the world's way of doing things, but that we should rather allow God to change us through renewing our thought patterns:

> *A* nd do not be conformed to this world, but be transformed by *the renewing of your mind, that you may prove what is that good and acceptable and perfect will of God.*

Romans 12:2

Paul is addressing the root of the problem here – our thinking and established thought patterns. He encourages us to think differently and no longer to see ourselves as sinners. You need to live with the assurance that you are the righteousness of God – completely innocent, a new creation, fully restored and appointed to rule and reign.

Christ is not just an example for me, but rather of me!
God's ideal for every person is that we would be who He originally created us to be. The only way you'll ever get this right is to discover each day who you are in Christ. The greatest and most liberating discovery I could make is that Christ is not only an example for me, but rather an

example of me. I'm no longer looking through the display window of a shop, for example, hoping to be like Him one day. I am now looking into a mirror and discovering that He is an example of me and that I look just like Him.

The most important thing you need to know about your Godly identity is that you act like Christ because you are, in essence, just like Him!

5

LIVE AS A NEW MAN!

There is always something special about a man and woman getting married. There is nothing like a beautiful wedding photo of a famous couple on the cover of a magazine to get the sales up. It is even noticeable on Facebook how the comments start rolling in when someone announces they are engaged.

In 2011 Prince William and Kate Middleton were joined in matrimony at a highly-traditional wedding ceremony, which the media referred to as the wedding of the century. As millions of people watched the ceremony, they found themselves caught up in the magic of the moment.

So much effort and attention goes into planning a wedding that you almost give a sigh of relief when the wedding day finally arrives and everything runs smoothly. Nevertheless, the wedding day and ceremony were never intended to be the *grand finalé* or highlight of the relationship. The preparations and long-awaited wedding day are not, therefore, the final destination, but rather the beginning and pronouncement of an expected *happily ever after*!

A call to intimacy

In the same way, our relationship with Christ is compared to that of a man and woman in an intimate love relationship, because God desires to have an intimate relationship with each one of us. God not only loves us, but is the origin and essence of love. Love is something which only really comes into its own when it is expressed in relationship to someone else, because love is, in essence, a declaration of value. You cannot love if you do not consider the object of your love valuable. God's love for man was the proof that He deemed us extremely valuable.

God made man to live in relationship with Him. Unfortunately, Adam's sin destroyed that intimacy. Death reigned as a result of his one crime; this death refers to the separation between God and man. This meant that man lost his purpose for living, because God was now far from him and all that remained was the overwhelming burden of guilt, shame and pain.

Since then, every man has been confronted with this internal vacuum which he consciously and sub-consciously tries to fill in all sorts of ways – whether it be searching for status, wealth, pleasure or even spiritual experiences outside of relationship with Christ. It doesn't matter what you try to fill this spiritual vacuum with: whether it is a new age spiritual cleansing programme, whether you try to draw spiritual power from your Zen garden, or attempt to climb the Himalayas on your hands and knees, you will never be internally satisfied until you are filled with God yourself. The Greek word for vacuum is *koilia*. This specific word was used when Jesus called out: "If anyone is thirsty, let him come to Me and streams of living water will flow from within him (*koilia*)" (see John 7:37-38). God desires more than anything that we experience this satisfaction in the very core of who we are. Yet it is impossible to achieve this in our own strength!

This is why Mankind needed a Saviour – someone who could transform our lives and restore our relationship with the Father. Jesus was willing to be that person!

The good news declares that we just have to believe in Christ and the finished work He carried out on the cross. This results in a transformed life. A whole new level of intimacy and fulfilment in my relationship with God flows from this act of faith. The revelation of God's unconditional favor is part of this discovery. My dedication and obedience now flows naturally from the realisation that God's favor is already on my life.

The curtain is torn

The moment Jesus died, the curtain of the temple in Jerusalem, the heart of the Jewish religious system, was torn in two. In order to understand the full implications of this, we first need to understand what that curtain symbolised. This curtain is what separated the Holy Place from the Most Holy Place in the temple. Only the high priest could enter the Most Holy Place once a year in order to ask forgiveness for the sins of the people. Nobody else was allowed to go in, otherwise they would surely die:

... and the Lord said to Moses: "Tell Aaron your brother not to come at just any time into the Holy Place inside the veil, before the mercy seat which is on the ark, lest he die; for I will appear in the cloud above the mercy seat.

Leviticus 16:2

The high priest needed to follow a very strict ritual before entering the Most Holy Place, otherwise he would also die. He first had to cleanse himself with water and clothe himself in his priestly garments. After that, he sacrificed a bull and took the blood of the bull along with a bowl of incense into the Most Holy Place.

He then took the blood and sprinkled it on the mercy seat – in this way he asked for forgiveness for himself. After that he had to repeat the entire procedure, but this time he had to sprinkle the blood of a goat on the mercy seat in order to ask for forgiveness for the sins of the entire nation.

After this, the high priest laid his blood-stained hands on the head of a second goat which symbolised placing the sins of the entire nation onto this goat. The goat was then sent into the wilderness to die. This goat was known as the scapegoat. Both goats would die, the one on the altar and the other in the harshness of the wilderness.

This entire ritual was symbolic of man's condition: he could choose to identify with the death of the goat on the altar, or he could choose to follow his own path and eventually be confronted with his own corruption – like the goat who was sent into the wilderness to die. The high priest brought the blood of the goat before God as penance for the people's sin. Everyone's sin was covered and they could all go home. This ritual took place once a year, every year.

But there came a day when another High Priest came and shed His own blood – His blood was good enough to eternally remove the sins of the people and not simply to cover them! The blood of Jesus paid the full price for everyone's sins for eternity:

> ... not that He should offer Himself often, as the high priest enters the Most Holy Place every year with blood of another – He then would have had to suffer often since the foundation of the world; but now, once at the end of the ages, He has appeared to put away sin by the sacrifice of Himself.

> **Hebrews 9:25-26**

Through this one perfect sacrifice, we are free once and for all! THE MESSAGE translates Hebrews 9:25-26 as follows:

> *H*e doesn't do this every year as the high priests did under the old plan with blood that was not their own; if that had been the case, he would have to sacrifice himself repeatedly throughout the course of history. But instead he sacrificed himself once and for all, summing up all the other sacrifices in this sacrifice of himself,

the final solution of sin.

License to sin?

Jesus was the scapegoat who took each one of our sins upon Himself and He was crucified at Golgotha, a hill outside the city. Jesus did not only take the sins of selected people upon Himself, but He paid for the totality of every sin committed by every single person who would ever live! For the first time since the fall of Adam, man was legally free from guilt and shame! This new blameless identity gives us the privilege of having an unhindered relationship with God.

When you gain the insight of having unhindered access to the throne of God, and once you've tasted the reality of having a relationship with the Author of life, you don't live as though you're trying to qualify for heaven. You then see sin and incorrect behaviour in a completely different light. Some people, and even some believers in their ignorance, see how much they can sin with the hope of still qualifying for heaven. *It is your sin that prevents you from getting into heaven, isn't it?* That is what many people believe. But the essential result of sin is not missing out on heaven. The result is separating ourselves from God and hindering the intimacy that is supposed to exist between us and God. It becomes the evidence of an identity not yet discovered. You are already missing out on heaven here on earth! Why would you only want something one day that you could already have now?

Jesus' death on the cross was by no means a license to carry on sinning! He did not die so we could simply carry on with our sinful habits without feeling any consequence for them whatsoever. Sin must be seen for what it is: the instrument that charged us with guilt and shame. Sin is most definitely not just a few things we did wrong which we need to quickly confess in order to escape punishment! Sin ruins the ability to enjoy and appreciate life in its fullness. Through sin we miss the original created purpose that Christ redeemed us for through His suffering – to discover our true identity, and to restore our intimate relationship with the Father.

While Jesus was on the cross, he cried out: "It is finished!" and the temple curtain was torn. This was a sign that we could access the presence of God with liberty. The offer was perfect and complete and it would never again be necessary for any man to have to pay penance for his sins.

After Jesus died, God the Father never said: "Everyone's sin is now forgiven; you can all go home and live like you want." No, the curtain was torn and the Father invited everyone to come inside to live a life of abundance. The crucifixion and resurrection of Jesus Christ was not the *grand finalé*. It was just the declaration of the beginning of a brand new life with God.

We are now welcome in the Most Holy Place because God, in Christ, cleansed us from all our sin and now sees us as cleansed in Christ. Our High Priest carried out a perfect and complete work on the cross and fully reconciled us with the Father. Our reward is not only heaven, but the privilege of having access to the presence of God. We do not work to qualify for it – even our attempt to uphold the law could not achieve it! Through Jesus Christ alone we have the privilege of entering His presence any time, without any fear or judgment in our hearts:

Yes, the old requirement about the priesthood was set aside because it was weak and useless. For the law never made anything perfect. But now we have confidence in a better hope, through which we draw near to God.

Hebrews 7:18-19, NLT

A new experience

We now have a different kind of relationship with Him to when we were sinners, because we have received a new identity. He illustrates His relationship with us as one between a father and son, or between a bride and bridegroom. In our relationship with God, we are no longer afraid of Him, although we do respect Him. We discover that God does not want to punish us, but that He really loves us. The lightning bolt of God's wrath against sin struck Jesus in my place and I now experience His favor on my life. God is definitely not just putting up with us, or keeping His distance from us; He rejoices over us - He delights in our salvation! God wants to reveal Himself to us as a loving father who accepts us unconditionally.

So you have not received a spirit that makes you fearful slaves. Instead, you received God's Spirit when he adopted you as his own children. Now we call him, "Abba, Father".

Romans 8:15, NLT

Paul uses the Aramaic word *abba* to describe this father-son relationship. It is a more intimate form of father – a word like "daddy", usually used by small children. Paul explains to the Ephesians that God desires to be a father to us:

But now in Christ Jesus you who once were far away have been brought near by the blood of Christ. For he himself is our peace, who has made the two groups one and has destroyed the barrier, the dividing wall of hostility, by setting aside in his flesh the law with its commands and regulations. His purpose was to create in himself one new humanity out of the two, thus making peace, and in one body to reconcile both of them to God through the cross, by which he put to death their hostility. He came and preached peace to you who were far away and peace to those who were near. For through him we both have access to the Father by one Spirit.

Ephesians 2:13-18, NIV

Unfortunately, not all of us have a healthy image of who and what a father is. For some people, the thought of God being a father is anything but pleasant. God wants to be the father to you that you may never have known or had. He wants to protect you and provide for you. He has planned an exciting future for you and has already made full provision for it. This is also why Jesus begins with "Our Father" when he is teaching us how to pray.

Christ came and gave His life for this. He made the love that was in the heart of the Father tangible for us – this is why you need to discover Christ's great love story in your own life. This discovery empowers us to live from a whole new framework of life.

The two cycles

Although our relationship with God is completely restored and we are able to live in that fullness today, the truth is people can sometimes get caught in feelings of guilt from time to time. People feel distant from God as a result of how they live.

We fall into a cycle of guilt when we miss the reality of intimacy with God. This is why it is essential to keep our focus on God's grace and His message of salvation so that we can keep enjoying intimacy with God.

The cycle of guilt

The cycle of guilt has three primary components: *conviction*, *condemnation* and *repentance*.

Firstly you become *convicted* of your sin and try to carry on

3. Repentence   **1.** Conviction

2. Condemnation

living as a better person, doing your best not to sin. You decide to do your best to live a blameless life. Before you know it, you do something wrong and end up disappointed in yourself.

This is when *condemnation* comes in and you feel ashamed and terrible about what you did wrong. You go back to feeling guilty and have no confidence to go before God. And then you revert to living the life you used to live before you met Jesus Christ.

The next step is to *repent*. You go to church on Sunday and it feels like the preacher is speaking directly to you. Your conscience is screaming at you and you decide to confess your sins and bring your shame to the Lord. You trust that He will forgive you and then you decide, once again, to go back to trying your best to live right!

This is the cycle that I, as a believer, experienced for years and I just accepted that this was the way it worked. We are taught, after all, to make quality decisions in life and to give our best. It sounds so pious and right, but deep down inside we all hope there is a better way.

All of us have been caught in this cycle at one point or another.

Each time we make the decision to live right, we stumble and feel guilty and repent once again. This cycle does not have a happy ending, because you constantly feel you are not good enough. This is precisely what the Old Covenant's way of living was based on. People needed to bring a sacrifice in order to pay for their sins. Although it averted God's punishment, the people could not get rid of the sense of guilt and this is what maintained the feeling of distance between them and God.

This is where the New Testament radically differs from the Old. The blood of Jesus has not only covered our sins, but it has totally washed them away, together with our guilt, in order to cleanse our conscience:

*B*ut Christ came as High Priest of the good things to come, with the greater and more perfect tabernacle not made with hands, that is, not of this creation. Not with the blood of goats and calves, but with His own blood He entered the Most Holy Place once for all, having obtained eternal redemption. For if the blood of bulls and goats and the ashes of a heifer, sprinkling the unclean, sanctifies for the purifying of the flesh, how much more shall the blood of Christ, who through the eternal Spirit offered Himself without spot to God, cleanse your conscience from dead works to serve the living God? And for this reason He is the Mediator of the new covenant, by means of death, for the redemption of the transgressions under the first covenant, that those who are called may receive the promise of the eternal inheritance.

Hebrews 9:11-15

The cycle of grace

Paul offers us a better way of doing things in the cycle of grace. This cycle has three components – *know*, *reckon* and *present* – which he illustrates to us in Romans 6.

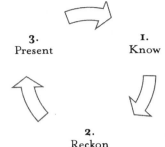

3.
Present

1.
Know

2.
Reckon

In verses 3, 6 and 9 he repeatedly uses the word "know", although he uses three different words, in this way showing the progressive understanding of knowing.

In verse 3: "... or do you not *know*?" This is the Greek word *agnoeo* which means to be ignorant.

In verse 6: "... but you know that your old man was crucified with Christ ..." This is the Greek word *ginosko* which means to *learn to know* or *come to the knowledge of*.

In verse 9: "... but we *know* ..." This is the Greek word *eido* which means to *see as a result of revelation* and *to be convinced...*

Paul makes it clear that our victory lies in the fact that we need to know something. This knowing is a process of understanding that systematically changes our old thought patterns so we can think and live in a new way.

What is this great insight we need to understand? That the old 'me' was crucified with Christ on the cross. My inferiority, guilt, shame and confusion were completely dealt with two thousand years ago. I no longer have to consider myself a poor, struggling sinner – because that is not who I am!

The fact that we still do the wrong things does not make us sinners. Paul says the reason we sometimes mess up is because we still struggle with a slave mentality. The old 'you' no longer exists because he is dead. This is an immense concept that you and I need to realise and know. It's all about who you are now! The sinful person you once were was crucified with Christ and you now live a new life in Him.

Jesus did so much more for us than just save us. We died with Him and were raised to a new life together with Him. If I cannot see myself with Jesus on the cross, the cross actually means nothing to me. The Bible says I have been crucified *with* Christ which is why I am able to think differently about myself and about sin:

For we know that our old self was crucified with him so that the body ruled by sin might be done away with, that we should no longer be slaves to sin.

Romans 6:6, NIV

We perceive that our old lifestyle was co-crucified together with him; this concludes that the vehicle that accommodat–

ed sin in us was scrapped and rendered entirely useless. Our slavery
to sin has come to an end.

Romans 6:6, THE MIRROR

Peter says the following about sin: "To return to sin is like a pig that has been cleaned and goes and rolls in the mud again, or like a dog that returns to its own vomit." (see 2 Peter 2:22). Why would you do that?

Paul confirms that we suffered with Christ on the cross, which is why we need to arm ourselves with the thought that we have ceased to sin. I Peter 4:1-2 puts it like this: "Therefore, since Christ suffered for us in the flesh, arm yourselves also with the same mind, for he who has suffered in the flesh has ceased from sin, that he no longer should live the rest of his time in the flesh for the lusts of men, but for the will of God." When you know you have been crucified with Christ and raised with Him, you become part of the cycle of grace that Paul continues to spell out for us:

L ikewise you also, reckon yourselves to be dead indeed to sin, but alive to God in Christ Jesus our Lord.

Romans 6:11

To reckon yourself dead to sin, is the Greek word *logizomai* which is where the word "logic" comes from. Therefore, what he is saying is that you should come to the logical conclusion that you are able to live a life of victory because you died and were raised with Christ. If you know this for a fact, reckon yourself dead to sin and alive to God! Paul says you must know, so that you can reckon, in order to come to the logical conclusion and present your members as instruments of righteousness and not instruments of sin.

The final step – *present* – means a resultant adjusting of your life; to establish things in your life differently so that you can live for God.

How does the cycle of grace work if you do something wrong? Instead of feeling condemned again, you need to remind yourself of what you know. What do you know? That the action of sin does not reflect who you truly are. That you are definitely not a sinner, but that you are in Christ and a new creation. This is your true identity now. Doing something wrong does not determine your identity – run to what you know you truly are!

You now understand who you are in Christ. You know you have been created to live permanently in intimacy with God and that you shouldn't run from Him if you do something wrong. This is why Paul exclaims:

There is therefore now no condemnation to those who are in Christ Jesus, who do not walk according to the flesh, but according to the Spirit.

Romans 8:1

You walk in the spirit by reminding yourself that you have a new identity in Christ and no longer see yourself as a sinner. You walk in the flesh when you associate yourself with Adam and see yourself once again as a poor old sinner.

When you function within the cycle of grace, there is absolutely nothing that can breach your intimacy with God and you are able to declare victoriously, "I have been designed and created for intimacy with God!"

6

NO MORE EFFORT

In the previous chapter we looked at how the cycle of grace works. Firstly, there is something you need to know in order to function within this cycle. You must know, and constantly remind yourself, that what Christ did on the cross was a finished work, which means that you are no longer a sinner, but the righteousness of God. You need to come to the realisation that you are dead to sin and alive to God!

Under the authority of the law

In Romans 7, it looks as though Paul completely forgets about the life of victory he spoke about in Romans 6. He is communicating here like someone who does not seem convinced that there is no condemnation for those who are in Christ – which is exactly what he later again so convincingly speaks about in Chapter 8! What happened in chapter 7 then? The key to Chapter 7 is found in the way Paul begins:

*O*r do you not know, brethren (for I speak to those who know the law), that the law has dominion over a man as long as he lives?

Romans 7:1

Paul, who was once a Pharisee himself, knew that the Jews had a deep desire to uphold the law. Many of the Jews turned to Christ for salvation and settled in other parts of the world. Some ended up in Rome where they wanted to mix their old legalistic practices with their newly-formed faith in Christ. This is why he asks them, "Do you remember how we used to live while we were still under the law?"

In taking his readers back to the time they were still living under the law, Paul reminds me of the story I once heard about a particular Statistics post graduate class.

A group of post graduate students, who were studying in a variety of biological fields, had Statistics as a shared subject. Despite the lecturer explaining the work to them to the best of his ability the students just could not master it.

It made no difference how the students tried to apply the formulas to the data, things just would not work out. They worked harder than they had ever worked before and attended extra classes, but by the third term the entire class's results were still not good enough for them to pass.

The end of the year drew closer and there was not much time to salvage anything positive. They approached their study leaders and eventually the problem landed on the university management's desk. To the great relief of the students, the head of the faculty decided to discontinue the subject and the students no longer had to attend classes. It was further announced that every student would receive a passing grade for the subject. The students were exempt from the subject, and all the fear that accompanied it disappeared.

Just like it felt completely impossible for these students to pass Statistics, the Jews also felt that it was not possible to uphold every aspect of the law. The law merely brought a sense of despair and fear. The Pharisees were so afraid they would break the law that they set other laws in place to ensure they would not break the original law.

One of the classic examples of this was the law concerning the Sabbath. Obviously the Pharisees believed that they were not permitted to work or do any kind of manual labour on the Sabbath. They had long discussions about precisely what it meant to work on the Sabbath. Work, they said, included ploughing, for example, which is why you were not permitted to plough on the Sabbath.

The next question was, of course, what it meant to plough. After a long debate it was decided that ploughing meant any form of furrowing in the ground. This just led to a further question – what does it mean to furrow in the ground? The Pharisees did not want to take any chances or create any opportunities to falter.

They then determined that one was also prohibited from spitting on the Sabbath, because imagine if one spat so hard that it resulted in a small furrow in the ground, which would then mean that one had ploughed. And if one ploughed, it meant one had worked, and if one worked on the Sabbath it meant the law had been broken! The Pharisees established hundreds of laws for themselves to ensure that their lives were set on fulfilling the law as carefully and accurately as possible. This was as meticulous as one could get!

Paul compares our life under the law with a marriage. He begins Romans 7 with the question: "Do you not know that the law has dominion over a man as long as he lives?" A man and a woman are bound to each other in marriage until one of them dies. As long as they are both alive, they are committed to each other, as is expected of them within a marriage.

When one of them dies, the other is set free from any obligations towards the partner who has died. Should the surviving man or woman get married to someone else, the commitment they shared with their first spouse would no longer apply and would have no effect on the second marriage.

According to Paul, the law works in exactly the same way. It holds a power over us and places severe claims on us. It is already a challenge to recite the Ten Commandments from memory, let alone fulfil them one hundred percent throughout one's entire life! Paul says that even he himself was not able to fulfil all the laws and rules the Pharisees added:

I don't really understand myself, for I want to do what is right, but I don't do it. Instead, I do what I hate.

Romans 7:15, NLT

Paul realised that even if he tried really hard, he would never get it right. It felt to him like he was held prisoner by a power that forced him to do the wrong things:

For the good that I will to do, I do not do; but the evil I will not to do, that I practice. Now if I do what I will not to do, it is no longer I who do it, but sin that dwells in me. I find then a law, that evil is present with me, the one who wills to do good.

Romans 7:19-21

Paul confirms the same principle to the church in Ephesus:

We were all part of a common pattern, swept along under a powerful invisible influence, a spirit-energy that adopted us as sons to its dictate through unbelief. Throughout that time ev-

ery one of us were warped and corrupted in our conduct snared in a
jumble of forbidden lusts, driven by the desires of the senses, totally
engaged in an expression of life ruled by mind games; it was as if a
twisted passion parented a universal breed of people.

Ephesians 2:2-3, THE MIRROR

The law could not free us from this disgrace. Not because the law was bad – in fact the New Testament confirms numerous times that the law is inherently good – but because man had a problem in fulfilling it. The law came to point out man's failure and inability to do so and make him aware of his need for a saviour:

What shall we say then? Is the law sin? Certainly not! On the contrary, I would not have known sin except through the law. For I would not have known covetousness unless the law had said, "You shall not covet." But sin, taking opportunity by the commandment, produced in me all manner of evil desire. For apart from the law sin was dead. I was alive once without the law, but when the commandment came, sin revived and I died. And the commandment, which was to bring life, I found to bring death. For sin, taking occasion by the commandment, deceived me, and by it killed me. Therefore the law is holy, and the commandment holy and just and good.

Romans 7:7-12

Jesus spoke to the multitudes one day to make sure that everybody understood how important it was to uphold the whole of the law and not just selected portions of the law. He told them that whoever broke just one of the law's commands and taught others to do the same, would be called least in the kingdom of God.

In the same way, whoever upheld all the commands of the law and taught others to do the same would be called greatest in the kingdom of heaven.

And just in case anyone thought it was possible at that stage for man to uphold the law or gain the favor of God with their own efforts, Jesus placed his trump card on the table:

> **"**You have heard that it was said to those of old, 'You shall not commit adultery.' But I say to you that whoever looks at a woman to lust for her has already committed adultery with her in his heart."
>
> *Matthew 5:27-28*

It was already difficult to uphold the law, and Jesus was now making it ten times more difficult! He made it clear – it is impossible to fulfil the law. Man was facing a huge dilemma!

Thank God!
Sin had such a hold over people that Paul, in identifying with man's fallen state, desperately cries out: "O, what a

miserable person I am! Who will free me from this life that is dominated by sin and death?" Fortunately he also gives the triumphant answer: "Thank God! The answer is in Jesus Christ our Lord." (See Romans 7;24-25, NLT).

Paul describes man's condition of hopelessness because he realises that he could never fulfil the law in his own strength (Romans 7), but then the revelation breaks open that he is able to do so in Christ.

Man's once-shameful state in Adam is cancelled out and Paul describes this new-found joy in man's new life and authority in Christ.

Jesus Christ is our Saviour! He died for us and you and I died with Him so we could be freed from all the rules we had to obey. Just like a wife is released from the requirements of her marriage when her husband dies, we too are freed from our shameful identity in Adam. We have a new identity in Christ, which enables us to now fulfil the legal requirements of the law.

For what the law could not do in that it was weak through the flesh, God did by sending His own Son in the likeness of sinful flesh, on account of sin: He condemned sin in the flesh, that the righteous requirement of the law might be fulfilled in us who do not walk according to the flesh but according to the Spirit.

Romans 8: 3-4

We no longer measure ourselves against the law, but we continuously refer to our new life in Christ.

What was the purpose of the law?

What purpose then does the law serve? It was added because of transgressions, till the Seed should come to whom the promise was made; and it was appointed through angels by the hand of a mediator.

Galatians 3:19

God's plan was never for us to fulfil the law in order to be declared righteous. The purpose of the law was to show us what sin is and to make us aware of the fact that we could not help sinning – this is why we needed a Saviour.

Paul says that the law actually caused us to sin even more – it awakened sin within us!

But sin, taking opportunity by the commandment, produced in me all manner of evil desire. For apart from the law sin was dead. I was alive once without the law, but when the commandment came, sin revived and I died. And the commandment, which was to bring life, I found to bring death. For sin, taking occasion by the commandment, deceived me, and by it killed me.

Romans 7:8-11

This is where we clearly see the difference between law and grace. Many people are unsure about the message of grace because they think it gives people a free license to sin. The fact is – it is only when you truly understand grace that you realise that grace teaches you to live a new life:

For the grace of God that brings salvation has appeared to all men, teaching us that, denying ungodliness and worldly lusts, we should live soberly, righteously, and godly in the present age ...

Titus 2:11-12

Grace teaches you to live differently – no longer from your own strength or efforts, but something happens to you when you discover that you are a new creation. It was the law that made you aware of sin and actually indirectly pointed you towards sin. A legalistic person's life is dominated by his constant battle to overcome sin. He is aware of every possible thing that could constitute sin and tries to avoid it at all costs. He just about walks on eggshells to make sure he does not sin. The person who flourishes in the grace of God delights himself in God – his whole focus and life is God!

If you drive on the N3 highway between Johannesburg and Durban in South Africa, you drive past various chicken farms. At one farm there is a huge billboard that reads, "Do not hoot, chickens are sleeping." For the duration of the long drive until that billboard is reached no driver feels the urgent need to lean on his hooter. But the minute the driver sees the billboard it's almost as though the desire to hoot is awakened in him. The rule that says you may not do something is the very thing that makes you want to do it!

God knew there was no way that the law could save us. The law was only there so we could become aware of our sin and in this way awaken in us an urgent need for a saviour. This Saviour was Jesus – we could only be redeemed by Him – and this redemption is applicable to everyone regardless of what you have or have not done. Every person who is in Christ is, therefore, totally and utterly freed from his own efforts and attempts.

Paul makes it very clear in this statement:

Therefore by the deeds of the law no flesh will be justified in His sight, for by the law is the knowledge of sin.

But now the righteousness of God apart from the law is revealed, being witnessed by the Law and the Prophets, even the righteousness of God, through faith in Jesus Christ, to all and on all who believe. For there is no difference...

Romans 3:20-22

A possible misunderstanding
When Paul tells us in Romans 7 of how he struggled not to do the things that were wrong, people incorrectly think

he is referring to himself as a follower of Christ or even a New Testament believer. Paul is actually comparing life under the law with the new life in Christ here. And in this, we can all identify with him.

When Paul says that he neglects to do that which he wants to do, and does that which he detests, it makes you feel absolutely powerless. Many people still refer to this scripture when they say, "You know, if Paul, the great apostle could not even get it right to live in victory, how do you think I'm going to get it right?"

We don't realise how this perspective has already made such a deep imprint in our belief and theology as a Christian community! We have adjusted our theology to our experience of failure, rather than making the Word of God the foundation and starting point of our lives.

Paul describes to us his life under the law. He tells us how pointless it is to try to uphold the requirements of the law in order to win God's favor. Throughout the ages, so many people have tried their best to uphold the law but nobody has been able to get it right because they were under the dominion of a power from which they could not free themselves.

The good news, however, is that we have been delivered from this power! Jesus Christ freed us from the hold it had over us. It is this truth we need to know, and the truth, Jesus said, will set us free.

Then Jesus said to those Jews who believed Him, "If you abide in My word, you are My disciples indeed. And you shall know the truth, and the truth shall make you free." They answered Him, "We are Abraham's descendants, and have never been in bondage to anyone. How can You say, 'You will be made free'?" Jesus answered them, "Most assuredly, I say to you, whoever commits sin is a slave of sin. And a slave does not abide in the house forever, but a son abides forever. Therefore if the Son makes you free, you shall be free indeed."

John 8:31-36

We therefore no longer find ourselves in the predicament of living under the law. We now live in victory with Christ! The truth is that we have been made free in Christ Jesus. We are the product of the crucifixion and resurrection of Jesus. The New Testament does not reveal a new, revised set of rules attempting to contradict the Ten Commandments. The New Testament is the revelation of man's true identity in Christ and our unhindered relationship with the Father.

For the law was given through Moses, but grace and truth came through Jesus Christ.

John 1:17

*A*nd of His fullness we have all received, grace upon grace.

John 1:16a

Against this harsh background of the law, with Moses representing man's sentence of guilt, Jesus Christ came and unveiled grace and truth! He is the manifestation of our completeness.

Free from the power and stronghold of sin

Some people think it is somehow devout to say, "Oh well, we all have our little vices!" As long as you keep tolerating them, they will stay your little vices. However, it is unwise to keep confessing this because Christ has already accomplished victory over those vices for you and me. In fact, the Apostle John says it so clearly:

*H*e who sins is of the devil, for the devil has sinned from the beginning. For this purpose the Son of God was manifested, that He might destroy the works of the devil. Whoever has been born of God does not sin, for His seed remains in him; and he cannot sin, because he has been born of God.

1 John 3: 8-9

Christ has freed me from the law of sin:

*F*or the law of the Spirit of life in Christ Jesus has made me free from the law of sin and death.

Romans 8:2

When the Bible refers to the law in this verse, it is referring to a power, a government or an authority. A law is always the extension of a government. The implementation of a law is directly related to the effectivity or authority of the government guarding over it.

On the South African highways you can clearly see boards marked with the number 120. This means that you are not permitted to drive faster than 120 kilometres per hour. This might well be the biggest revelation that some people may read in this book!

Should you drive faster than this and happen to drive through a speed trap, you will receive a fine because you disregarded a law. You can choose to ignore the fine and all the reminders you receive, but it won't take long for the authorities to subpoena you to appear in court. You can still protest against it, but it will result in you being arrested for your crime. That is how it is, in principle, for every country – the law represents an authority or government.

The Bible tells us that there was a power or authority that had control over our lives – this was the power of sin. Because I am now in Christ, sin no longer has power over me. There is no longer any power over me forcing me to do what is wrong. Our lives are no longer controlled by sin but by the Spirit of God.

Jesus Christ conquered the power of sin and He is now the final authority over my life. It is, therefore, no longer me trying to live a better life, but rather me having discovered who I am in Christ and the authority He has given me over sin:

God went for the jugular when he sent his own Son. He didn't deal with the problem as something remote and unimportant. In his Son, Jesus, he personally took on the human condition, entered the disordered mess of struggling humanity in order to set it right once and for all. The law code, weakened as it always was by fractured human nature, could never have done that. The law always ended up being used as a Band-Aid on sin instead of a deep healing of it. And now what the law code asked for but we couldn't deliver is accomplished as we, instead of redoubling our own efforts, simply embrace what the Spirit is doing in us.

Romans 8:2-4 THE MESSAGE

Under new management

We are now under new management – the management of God's Spirit. The things that sin forced me to do and the power it had over me have now been destroyed. I now live in God's undeserved goodness:

Sin is no longer your master, for you no longer live under the requirements of the law. Instead, you live under the freedom of God's grace.

Romans 6:14, NLT

The law gave sin its power and awakened the wrong things within me and caused me to do things I didn't want to do – and in the same way I didn't do the things I wanted to. In contrast, grace awakened the desire in me to live right. Yes, I make mistakes sometimes, but I now have a natural desire to do the right things:

For the grace of God has appeared that offers salvation to all people. It teaches us to say "No" to ungodliness and worldly passions, and to live self-controlled, upright and godly lives in this present age...

Titus 2:11-12, NIV

We are not called to argue, debate or defend a particular doctrine – we are called to reveal the truth. The truth is the discovery of who we are in Christ. This truth makes us completely and utterly free from any false or confused thoughts about how we should live.

I bear fruit naturally

What do you expect to find when you walk through an orange orchard during harvest time? The fresh scent of citrus, of course; the evidence of fruit on the orange trees! What do you expect to find with people who are born into the new life from above and who have received a new identity in Christ? You expect godly fruit – fruit that is produced naturally and spontaneously through the Christ within.

To bear fruit is different from doing works in response to an external law. Fruit is something that is produced spontaneously and naturally. Works are enforced externally. In order to do good works, you need to set alarms to remind you and think out punishments if you neglect to do them.

The fruit of the spirit – love, joy, peace, patience, kindness, goodness, faithfulness, gentleness and self-control – are all produced naturally and spontaneously from within us.

Think differently!

We now bear fruit in keeping with repentance. The Greek word for repentance is *metanoia* which means to *think differently*.

The Vulgate is one of the earliest and most widely used Latin translations of the Bible. This specific version translated the word *repentance* as *penance*. For centuries, people were under the impression that repentance meant confessing your sins and renouncing them. But *metanoia* means a radical change of thinking.

Metanoia is a compound word, coming from the two words, *together* and *think*. It, therefore, means to think together with God! This is the appeal of the Gospel – we need to think completely differently about ourselves, our circumstances and how we live.

Many churches have made penance or confession of sin the foundation of their faith, which binds people once again to guilt and condemnation. The message of salvation calls us to think and live together with God, with the expectation that we will bear fruit spontaneously because His thoughts are our thoughts.

You are now appointed to bear fruit that is fitting for someone who thinks differently about himself. Someone who thinks they are a sinner, thinks differently from someone who thinks they are the righteousness of God. See yourself the way God sees you. Paul refers to this in Romans 12:

And do not be conformed to this world, but be transformed by the renewing of your mind, that you may prove what is that good and acceptable and perfect will of God.

Romans 12:2

It is essential that our thoughts are constantly being renewed, otherwise we can easily fall back into the snare of condemnation. Unfortunately, the way we speak and the way we think are sometimes still a reflection of how we saw ourselves before we were in Christ. This kind of mind-set will just encourage our old thought patterns instead of focussing on the victory we have achieved in Christ.

As a child, I was afraid of God for years because I was convinced I needed to regularly do certain things in order to win His approval. I needed to live right all the time so that He would not become unhappy with me. I was relying on my own efforts to ensure that I went to heaven.

For years, we have preached a message from the pulpit that we are guilty and that God will punish us if we don't change. This results in people becoming anxious and asking what they need to do in order to avoid God's judgment. We then offer them the cycle of guilt and the first thing they need to do is repent.

In this case, repentance is not discovering my new position in Christ, but it is rather focussing my energy on my own failure and shame. Of course there is a brokenness evident in someone who realises he has done something wrong and wants to get his life right with God. There is nothing wrong with this. You cannot, however, stop at just saying sorry, you need to discover who you are in Christ and that He has freed you from your old ways of thinking and doing!

The enemy's plan is to keep you from discovering who you are in Christ at all costs. Identity determines behaviour (activity) – as long as you believe you are not worthy and can't help sinning, you will continue to disappoint yourself and, as a result, feel guilty and condemned.

Living in victory means surrendering to the work that was done on the cross. You need to know, see and understand. You need to know who you truly are and how God sees you now that you are in Christ. If you are in Christ, you are a new creation – you underwent an identity change; you are now a completely different person! You are no longer a sinner, but the righteousness of God!

There is no more condemnation; there is only redemption. Redemption brings confidence because you no longer feel guilty and you can experience an intimate relationship with God:

What then shall we say to these things?

If God is for us, who can be against us? He who did not spare His own Son, but delivered Him up for us all, how shall He not with Him also freely give us all things? Who shall bring a charge against God's elect? It is God who justifies. Who is he who condemns? It is Christ who died, and furthermore is also risen, who is even at the right hand of God, who also makes intercession for us. Who shall separate us from the love of Christ? Shall tribulation, or distress, or persecution, or famine, or nakedness, or peril, or sword?

As it is written: "For Your sake we are killed all day long; We are accounted as sheep for the slaughter."

Yet in all these things we are more than conquerors through Him

who loved us. For I am persuaded that neither death nor life, nor
angels nor principalities nor powers, nor things present nor things
to come, nor height nor depth, nor any other created thing, shall
be able to separate us from the love of God which is in Christ Jesus
our Lord.

Romans 8:31-39

Just like the case of the university management who intervened and provided a solution for the post graduate students that went way beyond their own limited ability to solve, Christ provided a way for me to be set free from my own limitations and the judgment of the law.

It would have been foolish if, after all this, one of the students turned up at the examination venue in order to write the exam, or doubted the pass mark he was given. Believe it or not – there are still "students" like this! In the same way, it would be foolish to doubt the finished work of the cross or to try to contribute something towards it.

Christ fulfilled the law on our behalf and obtained this complete victory for us. In Christ, I am once and for all exempt from any effort to uphold the law in order to gain the approval of God!

7

HEIRS OF A NEW TESTAMENT

The year was approximately 1400 BC – Jericho's walls had fallen and the city of Ai had been captured after a second attempt. Rumours concerning what happened in Jericho and Ai had spread like wildfire amongst the Canaanites. The Israelites were in the process of conquering the land God had promised them, and all the nations teamed up to fight against Israel – everyone except the Gibeonites, themselves residents of Canaan.

The Gibeonites heard that there was no-one who was able to conquer Israel and they came up with a cunning plan. They disguised themselves as travellers from a foreign land; they wore old shoes and old clothes and carried mouldy bread in their bags. They went to Joshua and the people looking worn-out and weary and begged them not to kill them but rather to enter into a covenant of peace with them. Without consulting God, Joshua incorrectly entered into a covenant of peace with the Canaanites.

Busted!

After the covenant was cut, the Israelites found out too late that their new covenant partners were actually Canaanites. God had commanded them to kill all the Canaanites but now it was too late to go back on their word. The Gibeonites had avoided death and now had the protection of Israel.

The king of Jerusalem heard that Israel was undefeated and also that the Gibeonites had entered into a covenant of peace with them*. The king then decided, along with a few other kings, to declare war on the Gibeonites. On the grounds of the covenant they had entered into with Israel, the Gibeonites asked Israel to stand with them and fight against the king of Jerusalem.

What happened that day was absolutely spectacular! God arrived on the scene and told Joshua not to be afraid and that He would deliver the enemy into his hand (see Joshua 10:8). God then sent massive hailstones that killed more people than the Israelites could kill with their swords! (See Joshua 9-10)

More than four hundred years later a huge drought hit the land while David reigned as king. David went to God and asked Him why there had been a drought in the land for three years. God simply answered that a covenant had been broken and that Saul had killed some of the Gibeonites (see 2 Samuel 21).

---

* At this time Jerusalem and Israel as a people were not united.

God still honoured the covenant between Israel and the Gibeonites four hundred years after it was entered into. Even though this covenant was made in a cunning manner, the principle remained that it was still a covenant that could under no circumstances be broken.

When parties enter into covenant

In the Bible we often read of God entering into covenant with people, or people entering into covenant with each other. The Hebrew word for covenant is the word *berith* which means an agreement. A covenant was not something you entered into easily or took lightly – it was the holiest and most solemn kind of agreement into which two parties could enter. This covenant was also binding until death separated the two parties.

There were certain steps that needed to be followed in order to enter into covenant:

1. The ceremony would begin with the exchange of cloaks. In ancient Biblical culture, your cloak represented your identity and, in effect, the two parties now represented each other.

2. After that, they would exchange belts and swords as a symbol of protection. So, if you and I were entering into a covenant in this way, the implication would be that all my power and ability was now available to you; should anyone attack you or take advantage of you, it was as good as them doing it to me.

3. The two parties would subsequently cut their palms and press their hands together in order for their blood to mix. They rubbed sand or ash into the wound so that there would be a lasting scar as proof of the covenant.

4. The next step was to slaughter an animal and cut it in two. The two pieces were then placed on the ground and both parties walked around and through them in a figure of eight – the symbol of infinity.

5. The two parties also exchanged names, which once again indicated that they represented each other.

6. The two parties then stood before each other and spoke out blessings and curses over each other – blessings which would follow if they kept the covenant and curses should the covenant be broken.

7. They then enjoyed a meal together. This meal was called the covenant meal and was enjoyed by the respective family members and witnesses.

8. Afterwards, they planted a tree, dug a well or even built an altar, which would serve as a reminder of the covenant for the generations to follow.

God's covenant with Abraham

In Genesis 15 we are told that God brought a deep sleep over Abraham and took him through the stages of covenant in a dream.

God promised Abraham many descendants – as many as the sand on the seashore and the stars in the heavens. God entered into a covenant with Abraham to confirm that what He promised would take place. Abraham needed to bring Him a calf, a goat, a ram, a turtledove and a young dove and then sacrifice them. God then blessed Abraham and confirmed that he would possess the land He would give to his descendants.

It was at this point that God changed Abram's name to Abraham (father of many nations). Since Abram and Sarai were unable to have any children of their own at that stage, this new name with its promise from God meant a lot to Abram. Sarai's name also changed. Where she was once known as the wife of Abram, her new name Sarah now included part of God's covenantal name. God places His covenant name YAHWEH within their new names. The Jews never wrote God's covenant name, YAHWEH, with vowels, thus preventing God's name from being used in vain. They, therefore, wrote the name as "YHW", using only consonants. It was this "h" sound that was incorporated into both of their names – Abra"h"am and Sara"h" – as proof of their covenant with God. From that day on, God chose to be known as the God of Abraham and later also of Isaac and Jacob.

The covenant with Israel is confirmed

God kept His part of the covenant and gave Abraham and Sarah a son of their own – Isaac, the son of the promise. Abraham's descendants multiplied, just as God had promised. A few hundred years later, Israel was free from slavery and was on the way to the land God had promised them – the land of milk and honey!

On the way to the Promised Land Moses reminded the Israelites about the covenant God had made with them. He wrote everything down that the Lord had commanded them and built an altar where the Israelites could bring offerings to the Lord:

Then he took the Book of the Covenant and read in the hearing of the people. And they said, "All that the Lord has said we will do, and be obedient." And Moses took the blood, sprinkled it on the people, and said, "This is the blood of the covenant which the Lord has made with you according to all these words."

Exodus 24:7-8

In this way, God renewed the covenant He had made with Israel with the new generation. This was, however, not the last time. In Deuteronomy 28 the process was repeated again and God gave a long list of blessings Israel would receive if they upheld their part of the covenant.

Later, as we read on, we see an even longer list of curses that would come over the people if they did not obey everything God had commanded. After everything had been clearly spelled out, Moses told the people:

Therefore keep the words of this covenant, and do them, that you may prosper in all that you do.

Deuteronomy 29:9

The conditions of blessing

All these wonderful blessings were available to Israel on condition that they were fully obedient; fulfilled the law and all its ordinances; and did what was required. If not, they would be cursed.

The blessings included that they were the head and not the tail; that they would be blessed in the field, in their homes and in every area of their lives. All these blessings, however, were subject to all the conditions laid out in the law, and as we already know, this was impossible for the Israelites to fulfil.

Receiving the blessings was, therefore, based on the principle of covenant: each party had a share they had to perform. It was also not something that was taken lightly and for this reason it was essential that both parties upheld the agreement.

This is precisely the problem Israel was sitting with – they did not have the ability to fulfil their part of the covenant, regardless of how hard they tried. As a result of the hold sin had on man, they could not meet the requirements of the covenant. Consequently, the Israelites did not experience too many of these blessings and they needed to protect themselves against the curses. Where the covenant was supposed to be a means to blessing, it had become a means to a curse. The Israelites would thus have been a cursed nation had it not been for the sin offerings that temporarily covered their sins.

The curse of the law

Man could not succeed in living like this, which is why this covenant, regulated by the law, became a curse for him:

For as many as are of the works of the law are under the curse; for it is written, "Cursed is everyone who does not continue in all things which are written in the book of the law, to do them." But that no one is justified by the law in the sight of God is evident, for "the just shall live by faith."

Galatians 3:10-11

The law came to show man that he was an unworthy, fallen being (as a result of the fall) who needed a saviour – in essence it placed a magnifying glass on his sinful nature. This is why Scripture tells us that sin gained entry into our lives when the law was introduced, because only then could man truly realise how sinful he was:

But now we have been delivered from the law, having died to what we were held by, so that we should serve in the newness of the Spirit and not in the oldness of the letter. What shall we

say then? Is the law sin? Certainly not! On the contrary, I would
not have known sin except through the law. For I would not have
known covetousness unless the law had said, "You shall not covet."
But sin, taking opportunity by the commandment, produced in me
all manner of evil desire. For apart from the law sin was dead.

Romans 7:6-8

It is important to remember that the law is not bad – it never was. The law is complete and represents God's standard of life – it was God's description of how He wanted man to live. The law represents the perfect order of any society.

The law could not make us better people – it came to show us that we could do nothing to improve ourselves in order to win God's favor. This is why we needed someone to save us!

Time for a new covenant

After years of stumbling and getting up again, and stumbling again and getting up again, there is light at the end of the tunnel when the prophet Jeremiah prophesies the following:

❝The day is coming," says the Lord, "when I will make a new covenant with the people of Israel and Judah. This covenant will not be like the one I made with their ancestors when I took them by the hand and brought them out of the land of Egypt. They broke that covenant, though I loved them as a husband loves his

142

wife," says the Lord.

Jeremiah 31:31-32, NLT

❝*And I will forgive their wickedness, and I will never again re-member their sins."*

Jeremiah 31:34b, NLT

As a result of his sinful nature, the conditions of the old covenant were impossible for man to fulfil. It was time for a new covenant … it was time for a new testament.

The new "Testament"

The word for testament is the Greek word *diatheke* which means "inheritance" as opposed to the Hebrew word *berith* which primarily indicates an "agreement". The English translation of the Bible uses the words "covenant" and "testament" as alternating terms as though they are synonyms, but a covenant and a testament essentially differ in meaning. An agreement spells out what both parties have to do and not do, while a testament or will is a reference indicating who inherits what when someone dies.

A testament is only valid when the person, or testator, who drew it up, dies. The writer of Hebrews says that the New Testament works on the same principle:

*A*nd for this reason He is the Mediator of the new covenant, by means of death, for the redemption of the transgressions under the first covenant, that those who are called may receive the promise of the eternal inheritance. For where there is a testament, there must also of necessity be the death of the testator. For a testament is in force after men are dead, since it has no power at all while the testator lives.

Hebrews 9:15-17

If Jesus had not died we would not have inherited the fullness of God. While Jesus was on the earth, He knew there would be a day where He would have to die on a cross on behalf of all men. You could almost say He was born in order to die.

The night before He was handed over to die, He broke bread and took the cup and poured wine for his disciples. After that he announced His death with these words:

*T*hen He took the cup, and gave thanks, and gave it to them, saying, "Drink from it, all of you. For this is My blood of the new covenant, which is shed for many for the remission of sins."

Matthew 26:27-28

It is easy to understand these scriptures today because many of us have heard them since we were children. Jesus' disciples, however, did not understand what He was trying to tell them, because in their minds they were simply preparing to celebrate another Passover. The Passover was the anniversary of that night when the lamb that was slaughtered in Egypt brought about their forefathers' freedom from slavery. They probably wondered why, at this occasion, Jesus would say that this was now the New Testament in His blood? They had absolutely no comprehension of the fact that the one perfect price that would affect the salvation of the whole of mankind would take place within a few hours of their hearing this; a deliverance that would legally make every man an heir of God. Everything would change, a whole new dispensation would be announced – this was the dispensation that the law and the prophets so eagerly awaited!

Time for a new priestly order

Implementing this New Testament was simple. In the Old Covenant the priests acted as agents to keep the covenant. The law was the means of keeping this covenant intact. The priests, therefore, had to know the law and guard over it. Should the covenant change in any way, the priestly order and the law would be forced to change as well.

For when the priesthood is changed, the law must be changed also.

Hebrews 7:12, NIV

Up to the time of Jesus, all the priests came from the tribe of Levi and were responsible for preserving the priestly order. This order needed to function in a certain way and the framework of the order that needed to be implemented was known as the Law of Moses.

Amongst other things, this law determined that the high priest would enter the Most Holy Place once a year in order to offer atonement for the sins of the people. The high priest would do so by sprinkling the blood of a ram onto the Ark of the Covenant. The Levitical priesthood was by no means authorised to take away the sins of the people; their sins could merely be covered. This is why it was time for a new priest, from a new priesthood, with a new law, that would take away the sins of mankind once and for all.

Therefore, if perfection were through the Levitical priesthood (for under it the people received the law), what further need was there that another priest should rise according to the order of Melchizedek, and not be called according to the order of Aaron? For the priesthood being changed, of necessity there is also a change of the law.

Hebrews 7:11-12

The new priest was Jesus Christ and He was not a priest in the order of Aaron. Aaron also descended from the tribe of Levi and was appointed to carry out the priestly duties of the whole tribe. Jesus Christ was a priest in the order of Melchizedek. Melchizedek is the combination of two Hebrew words: *melek*, meaning king, and *tsedek*, meaning righteousness. Melchizedek was, therefore, the king of righteousness, the priestly king of righteousness and peace. Melchizedek was a type of Christ and some theologians claim that he was Jesus Himself.

We read about Melchizedek for the first time in Genesis 14 when he appeared to Abraham and shared the bread and wine with him. He blessed Abraham and, out of gratitude, Abraham gave him a tenth of all his money.

This Melchizedek, who appeared to Abraham, was the king of *Salem* (a city whose name meant peace) and the priest of the Almighty God. He was the only person ever to be both king and priest – in the Old Covenant you could only be one or the other.

For this Melchizedek, king of Salem, priest of the Most High God, who met Abraham returning from the slaughter of the kings and blessed him, to whom also Abraham gave a tenth part of all, first being translated "king of righteousness," and then also king of Salem, meaning "king of peace," without father, without mother, without genealogy, having neither beginning of days nor end of life, but made like the Son of God, remains a priest continually.

Hebrews 7:1-3

Melchizedek was also not part of a priestly order. In other words, Melchizedek did not take over the priesthood from anyone or hand it over to anyone. He also had no natural mother or father – we can, therefore, deduce that he was nobody else but Christ Himself!

Christ became the king and priest in the order of Melchizedek – king and priest of righteousness and peace. Even David prophesied about this new priestly order in Psalm 110:4 ... "The Lord has sworn, And will not relent, 'You are a priest forever according to the order of Melchizedek'." Christ is, therefore, not a priest in the order of Aaron, from the tribe of Levi like all the other priests, but He was born from the tribe of Judah, appointed by His heavenly Father as High Priest in the order of Melchizedek (see Psalm 110:1-4).

When the priesthood changed, the law also needed to change

The Law of Moses, where man was thoroughly aware of his own efforts, needed to make way for grace – the dispensation where the favor of God undeservedly rested on men. The righteousness Christ accomplished for us was made possible by the power of His indestructible life and not because He was born from the correct tribe, as was required by the Law of Moses.

For the priest we are talking about belongs to a different tribe, whose members have never served at the altar as priests. What I mean is, our Lord came from the tribe of Judah, and Moses never mentioned priests coming from that tribe. This change has been made very clear since a different priest, who is like Melchizedek, has appeared. Jesus became a priest, not by meeting the physical requirement of belonging to the tribe of Levi, but by the power of a life that cannot be destroyed.

Hebrews 7:13-16, NLT

Jesus, our high priest, cried out the following words just before He let out His final breath: "It is finished!" His mission to save the world was complete. The agreement or covenant God had with us to fulfil the law had now been declared null and void and a new covenant was entered into – one where blessing was guaranteed through the finished work of His Son.

The moment Jesus died His testament was validated and we became the legal heirs of everything He left for us in it. It is essential to understand that this is the mystery that had been hidden away in God's heart through all the ages!

The inheritance of a new testament

Through dying for us on the cross Jesus bore every curse that had come over us from not upholding the law, and every blessing that was promised to Abraham was now part of our inheritance:

Christ has redeemed us from the curse of the law, having be- come a curse for us (for it is written, "Cursed is everyone who

hangs on a tree"), that the blessing of Abraham might come upon
the Gentiles in Christ Jesus, that we might receive the promise of the
Spirit through faith.

Galatians 3:13-14

All these blessings are part of the blessing and inheritance
we received in Christ. The Old Covenant is no longer valid;
you are no longer only blessed when you do certain things,
you are blessed because you are in Christ!

The gospel many people preach is still based on Deuteronomy 28, which says that if you do this, then God will do
that. There is no longer any kind of agreement between
you and God that stipulates what you must do – you are
now part of His covenant of grace!

You also no longer have to stare at all the curses in Deuteronomy 28 with fear. Christ became the curse so that you
could be blessed. You have inherited all the blessings listed
in Deuteronomy 28 without doing anything in order to
deserve it. Yes, you will be blessed in the city; and blessed
in the field; the work of your hands will be blessed, along
with your property and all your money!

Tension between the law and the grace of God

Finally, it is important to understand that the law is not
bad. Many people experience tension regarding law and
grace and how we should understand the difference. We
must remember that we have been taught from a young age

to carry out the law. Our framework was the Ten Commandments and many times we want to hang onto this because it gives us some kind of religious security. Once we understand that the law is not able to contribute to our salvation in any way and also could never cause us to earn God's approval, we open the door to a better way to God.

The law is inherently good, but it is not the foundation of our relationship with God. In fact, if we do not choose to turn away from the law as the basis for our salvation, we will never be free.

*A*nd we have such trust through Christ toward God. Not that we are sufficient of ourselves to think of anything as being from ourselves, but our sufficiency is from God, who also made us sufficient as ministers of the new covenant, not of the letter but of the Spirit; for the letter kills, but the Spirit gives life.

2 Corinthians 3:4-6

We are able to live a life of abundance when we stop trying to earn God's favor. I am not "doing" so that I can "become". I must discover that I "am" so that I can live in that truth. Until I recognise this, a veil or a covering will remain over my thoughts. We need to discover that the Old Covenant has been declared void!

As long as the law is our focus we are blinded

*B*ut *their minds were blinded. For until this day the same veil remains unlifted in the reading of the Old Testament, because the veil is taken away in Christ. But even to this day, when Moses is read, a veil lies on their heart. Nevertheless when one turns to the Lord, the veil is taken away. Now the Lord is the Spirit; and where the Spirit of the Lord is, there is liberty. But we all, with unveiled face, beholding as in a mirror the glory of the Lord, are being transformed into the same image from glory to glory, just as by the Spirit of the Lord.*

2 Corinthians 3:14-18
This discovery gives me the opportunity to discover the life God intended me to live.

I now discover – as in a mirror – who I truly am. He is the mirror image of my true identity and His glory now becomes the definition of my existence. This is the message of the New Testament and also the key to discovering our new identity in Christ. Our inheritance is locked up in the discovery of who we really are. Jesus Christ came to announce this insight into our lives.

God's plan for us is locked up in the testament, the inheritance – which by implication means that we are now blessed of God. All that we need to do is just believe that we are included in the finished work on the cross.

This new life of discovering our inheritance, repositions our entire outlook on life – how we think, speak and how we behave!

8

DO YOU STILL MIX THE OLD COVENANT WITH THE NEW TESTAMENT?

Expect God's supernatural working in your life today – then you'll see how your life changes completely! Our expectation for the future can sometimes be totally negative and so full of anxiety because we focus on our current circumstances. Like Abraham, the father of faith, we need to learn to look past our natural senses and to focus on a new and positive expectation.

The Lord wants to awaken in us a new expectation for the future. This expectation is not based on our performance, but in the confidence that through His Son, God has pronounced His favor over our lives. If our expectation is in line with God's pronouncement of favor, He will meet us at the level of our expectation. This creates an atmosphere for the supernatural work of God, which then becomes visible in our lives.

In chapter 7 we looked at both the scope and implications of a covenant with God, which by implication means that He will bless me as long as I do what He says. The focus was on me and my ability to uphold the law in order to become saved and blessed. In contrast, the New Testament announces what God accomplished through Christ, declaring that I became an heir when Christ died. The focus is on Christ and what He did on the cross for me.

Unfortunately, some people have the tendency to mix the human requirements of the Old Covenant with the New Testament's framework of grace. This places people under the power of the law once again and negates the power of the New Testament.

Levi and Judah

The Law of Moses determined that all the Old Covenant priests had to descend from the tribe of Levi. They then became part of the priesthood of Aaron. But Christ came from a completely different tribe and He became a high priest from a different priestly order.

When you look at the history of Levi and Judah, you realise that it is definitely not a coincidence that Jesus was born from the tribe of Judah and not from the tribe of Levi. It had everything to do with the circumstances in which Levi and Judah were born. In order to understand this, we need to go back to Jacob, the father of Levi and Judah.

Jacob fled from his home and his family and went to work for his uncle, Laban. In Genesis 29 we read that Laban said to him: "Because you are my relative, should you therefore serve me for nothing? Tell me, what should your wages be?" Laban had two daughters, but Jacob found Rachel the most beautiful. He asked Laban if he could marry Rachel if he worked for him for seven years.

Seven years went by and Scripture says it felt to him like a few days because he was so in love with Rachel. The big day finally arrived when Jacob was permitted to marry Rachel. Laban, however, tricked him and gave him Leah, his eldest daughter, as a wife instead. I'm not sure how things worked practically in those days, but Jacob only discovered that he had married the wrong woman after his first night of being married.

Of course, Jacob protested the matter with his father-in-law. Laban explained that it was custom to first give the elder daughter away in marriage, but that he would accommodate Jacob by giving him Rachel as a wife as well. Jacob thus became the husband of two wives – he loved the one with all his heart and he put up with the other one. The problem was that the wife he loved was not able to bear him children.

It was extremely important for a man in those days to have offspring, which is why it was necessary for sons to be born from a marriage. In order for a wife to gain the favor of her husband, she needed to preferably produce at least three sons. God blessed Leah with the ability to have children. The fact that Rachel could not have children was, therefore, a great opportunity for Leah to win Jacob's favor and love.

We read about this in Genesis 29:32;

So Leah conceived and bore a son, and she called his name Reuben; for she said, "The Lord has surely looked on my affliction. Now therefore, my husband will love me."

Leah fell pregnant again, brought a son into the world and said: "Because the Lord has heard that I am unloved, He has therefore given me this son also." She named him Simeon (meaning: 'God has taken notice of me'). Again she fell pregnant, again bringing a son into the world. This time she said: "Now this time my husband will become attached to me, because I have borne him three sons." This is why she named her son Levi.

Leah was so grateful she was able to bear Jacob three sons because she was convinced that he would now look at her differently. Leah expected to gain more favor from her husband due to the fact that she was able to bear him a third son, Levi. Can you see that Levi was born as an attempt to earn favor? In the birth and naming of Levi, this principle of performance was established. And this attempt to win love and approval would be continued in the Levitical priesthood.

It was not, however, the end of the story. A new day dawned for Leah:

*A*nd she conceived again and bore a son, and said, "Now I will praise the Lord." Therefore she called his name Judah. Then she stopped bearing.

Genesis 29:35

She named him Judah, which means *this time I will praise the Lord* or *praise*. The birth of this son had nothing to do with her need to perform to gain her husband's favor, acceptance and approval. She was so overwhelmed with God's goodness and grace that she spontaneously began to thank and praise Him.

In the naming of Judah, the principle of undeserved favor and grace is established.

Levi represents own works and performance, while Judah represents praise and the undeserved favor of God. The difference between Judah and Levi is the exact difference between the Old Covenant and the New Testament.

Old Testament = Levi: Came through the priesthood of Aaron.

The power or authority of the Law of Moses lies in the Ten Commandments which we need to uphold to please God so that He will bless us.

New Testament = Judah: Came through Jesus Christ and the priesthood of Melchizedek. The power or authority of the Law of Faith lies in believing that God has already blessed me in Christ.

The reality of this truth is that we do not live according to the Levitical priesthood, where we have to work for God's favor, but rather according to that which our high priest, Jesus Christ, already accomplished for us. Our calling is to respond to this with praise!

Any doctrine which emphasises good works and man's contribution to ensure salvation, is still part of the old dispensation. Trying to uphold the law requires more discipline and effort to win God's favor.

God's plan of salvation to reconcile us to Himself once again differentiates the true Christian faith from every other form of religion, including the Old Covenant. It is not about man's attempts to win the attention and favor of the Godhead.

The Good News is all about how God succeeded in putting an end to the enmity that existed between Himself and man, and to reconcile us to Himself.

For if when we were enemies we were reconciled to God through the death of His Son, much more, having been reconciled, we shall be saved by His life.

Romans 5:10

In the New Testament, there is no question of having to do anything in order to please God. The only thing that pleases God now is our faith.

God accomplished our salvation Himself. Our salvation is not hanging in the balance ... it is already a done deal! God is not still trying to decide if He is going to save us or not. God's love for us and the fact that He sent His only begotten Son, is the foundation of our faith.

By grace, God gave us everything as a gift! It is no longer necessary that we try to perform to win the favor of God. Instead, it insults the finished work of Christ if we still want to attempt to earn it ourselves. For then you are trying to do what Christ has already done for you.

Paul writes in his letter to the Galatians that if it had been at all possible to contribute anything in our own effort to our salvation, Christ died for nothing:

I do not set aside the grace of God; for if righteousness comes through the law, then Christ died in vain.

Galatians 2:21

It is, therefore, not about our diligence, but it is about the finished work Christ carried out for us. This understanding is so much more powerful than exercising our willpower! So many Christians still want to contribute something towards their qualification before God through their own spiritual commitment.

But like Leah, we have so many reasons to break out in praise to God.

In the same way that our High Priest from the tribe of Judah replaced the priests from the tribe of Levi, God replaced the Old Covenant with the New Testament. The dispensation of the Old Covenant is something of the past and it is most foolish to still want to live according to it.

Take, for example, the faithful old 286 IBM computer which has been out of use for at least twenty years. This computer had a hard drive memory of 6.5MB and worked at a speed of 10 MHz. In addition, it could take a "floppy" disk that stored a maximum of 8MB worth of data. The computer's total memory was more or less the equivalent of one or two files currently on my computer.

Now, why on earth would I give up my MacBook Pro in order to work on a 286 IBM computer? Why would you want to go back to something that does not work for you? As much as it is pointless and foolish to choose an old computer above something a lot better, it is pointless to go back to the old dispensation when Christ has made a new way for us!

This is why we want to tell the world that God has already accomplished our full salvation! God is not going to do anything else to deliver and empower the world – He has already done it.

Our redemption is complete in Christ

Scripture tells us that when the temple of Solomon was being built, there was no sound of a hammer or chisel on the Temple site, because everything had been finished in the quarry. This is the story of our salvation! We don't try to correct people's behaviour with hammers and chisels so that they can be good Christians through their committed human labour.

Unfortunately, we often try to make people Disciples of Christ by trying to change their behaviour. We like to give people all kinds of helpful steps to get them on the right track … but our best efforts only bring disappointment once more.

We need to be freed from having zeal for God and discover the zeal of God! God completely transformed or re-created us in the "quarry", or in other words, on the cross. What does this mean? It means essentially that there is no more change needed in your life – we're not going to try to beat you with a hammer and chisel until your life is right. You need to begin to discover and see yourself in Christ – you need to discover your perfection in Him, and then become who and what you already are!

We do not have enough time or enough courses to effectively change people's behaviour in this lifetime. What then can we do to change people's behaviour? We need to introduce them to their true identity – to Christ – so that they can discover who they really are. When a person grasps this revelation it changes the way they live. Why would you continue trying to fulfil a set of rules and regulations in your own strength when you know it is impossible for you to get it right?

Why would you choose the law over grace? As foolish as it might seem, this is exactly what a group of Jewish Christians did in Galatia – there are even people today who think this is the message of the Gospel.

Paul addresses the Galatians

The church in Galatia believed in Christ, but they also believed they needed to continue to fulfil the Law of Moses. They really wanted to do all they could to show they were devoted to the Lord, but it resulted in them becoming legalistic.

This is why Paul addressed them so harshly:

O *foolish Galatians! Who has bewitched you that you should not obey the truth, before whose eyes Jesus Christ was clearly*

*portrayed among you as crucified? This only I want to learn from
you: Did you receive the Spirit by the works of the law, or by the
hearing of faith? Are you so foolish? Having begun in the Spirit,
are you now being made perfect by the flesh?*

Galatians 3:1-3

When Paul finds that the Galatians have fallen into an
old mindset, he doesn't hold back! "Who has bewitched
you?" he asks.

He sounds desperate when he says later on:

*… how I wish I could be with you now and change my tone, because
I am perplexed about you!*

Galatians 4:20, NIV

You almost want to stop Paul and remind him that these
are actually good people – people who are devoted to God.
But these are the very people for whom Paul despairs.

The Message emphasises how strongly Paul feels about this:

*Are you going to continue this craziness? For only crazy people
would think they could complete by their own efforts what was*

begun by God. If you weren't smart enough or strong enough to begin it, how do you suppose you could perfect it?

Galatians 3:3, THE MESSAGE

But why is Paul so angry with them? He wasn't even this angry with the Christians in Corinth who were guilty of unthinkable sexual perversions and who freely challenged each other in court. You would think that if there was a church that needed sorting out, it would rather be the church in Corinth!

Something does not make sense – the Corinthians lived in sin and the Galatians were doing their best to live according to God's standards. Paul was patient with the Corinthians, because they were still ignorant concerning their position in Christ, but he was furious with the Galatians because they should have known better – yet they carried on mixing the legalistic approach of personal performance with the New Testament.

Perhaps it is because Paul came to the intense realisation that religiosity can be more dangerous than blatant sinfulness. The Galatians were saved because they believed, but now they wanted to continue living their spiritual lives by relying on their own efforts. Once again they placed all sorts of customs and requirements on people that served as conditions as to how spiritual they were.

Could it be that religiosity is worse than sin? Someone living in sin at least knows he/she is on the wrong track, but religion soothes your conscience, it even makes you proud and tells you that you're on the right track. You are convinced that living a good life makes you a righteous person. This may sound so right, but it is so wrong!

This is why Paul responded to the Galatians so fiercely. It is dangerous when someone believes and lives out a mixed message. On the one hand, you can't believe Christ has already done everything for you, and on the other hand you believe you still need to contribute something to qualify in order to be accepted by God.

Even the apostle Peter was guilty of mixing the Old Covenant with the New Testament – albeit sub-consciously:

> *But when Peter came to Antioch, I had to oppose him to his face, for what he did was very wrong. When he first arrived, he ate with the Gentile Christians, who were not circumcised. But afterward, when some friends of James came, Peter wouldn't eat with the Gentiles anymore. He was afraid of criticism from these people who insisted on the necessity of circumcision.*
>
> **Galatians 2:11-12, *NLT***

Early on in his ministry, Peter had a vision in which God commanded him to eat both clean and unclean animals (see Acts 10:9-16). Peter initially refused to do so, which is why God repeated the command. Peter could eat the unclean animals because God had declared them to be clean.

Further on we read how Peter ministered the gospel to Gentiles for the first time. Peter didn't seem to have a problem then of eating unclean animals with the Gentile Christians. Later on, however, Peter began to withdraw from meal times with the Gentile Christians because of them eating unclean animals.

The Jewish Christians believed in the crucifixion and resurrection of Jesus Christ, but they also believed they had to obey certain laws, for example not eating unclean animals.

Peter knew that nobody could earn God's favor any longer through obeying laws. However, he did not want to offend the Jewish Christians by preventing them from following Jewish customs.

Paul, however, was not inclined to this at all as he saw it as mixing the Old Covenant and the New Testament. If these are mixed, the result is dead religion. This is why Paul was so against it.

The danger of mixing the two is best explained in this following example: Bleach has the ability to remove stains from clothing, but sometimes the stains do not go away and all that remains are yellow marks. There is another way of removing stains – by using vinegar. Not many people know about this, which is why it is definitely not the first thing you grab when you come across a dirty mark. Imagine for a moment that you'd like to try the vinegar, but you also want to combine it with a little of what you're used to (the bleach) just to make one hundred percent sure that it works effectively. The question that invariably comes up is: can't I just mix the two? But if you happen to mix these two substances, it forms a poisonous gas called chloride gas. It attacks the mucus cells in your eyes and nose and it can be deadly. And so, if you wanted to combine these two cleaning agents, you would have a highly dangerous product with no cleaning ability.

The law sometimes makes me think of bleach. It is something we are used to and something we have been taught to use from a very young age. Despite the fact that you would never get it right to use it properly, at least you feel comfortable with it. The vinegar makes me think of the new plan God set in motion for us. This plan does not require any good works or establish any conditions and is by far the better plan. Yet it seems as though we cannot believe in its perfection and tend to quickly go back to what we know – our own ability in an attempt to gain God's favor.

Even though we want to mix the two, combining the best of both in order to make sure we're covered from all sides, we are deeming the grace of God to be less worthy than it is and we are engaged in a very dangerous doctrine. We cannot mix our own efforts with the finished work of Christ.

Jesus Christ is the only benchmark of God's favor and love for man. Jesus Christ is the worth that God attaches to each person!

Paul is fiery in his letter to the Galatians. He so desires that Christ would be formed in them and that they would live by faith again. When you live by faith, you change spontaneously.

We have tried to tell people for years that they just need to sort themselves out. This is about as helpful as trying to pick yourself up by your own shoelaces!

Faith is the fruit of the revelation of who Christ is and what He has done for you. If you realise the value that Christ has placed in you because He is in you, it will radically transform your thought patterns. Salvation is solely by grace, without any contributions from our side. Not even faith comes from us, but God's belief in our salvation places us in a position to believe, and this is His gift to us. His love for His Son is His love for us; He overwhelms us with the same favor!

When you realise this truth and allow this good news to become established in your heart, faith is something that happens spontaneously – as is the desire to obey God. Legalistic obedience limits you to your own fallible attempts and it only brings frustration and condemnation with it. Faith is the confidence in the infallible achievement of Christ – He performed on behalf of you and me. The fact that He was obedient even to death, effected every man's freedom.

My actions now become the natural fruit of my understanding of the Gospel. My understanding inspires what I do. Paul pleads with the church in Galatia to come to the knowledge of the truth. He is serious about bringing them to repentance and to point out their error, which is why he tells them a story to make the grace of God more comprehensible to them.

Isaac and Ishmael

God promised Abraham a son, but when it didn't look like it was going to happen, Abraham agreed with Sarah that he would take Hagar as his concubine. Hagar fell pregnant and Ishmael was born.

Their joy, however, did not last long because God told Abraham that Ishmael was not the son He had promised. Ishmael was already a teenager when Sarah finally fell pregnant and gave birth to Isaac, the son of the promise. I can just imagine how much joy and gladness accompanied this birth!

After a two year period, it was time for Isaac to be weaned and Abraham organised a huge feast. Before the event, Ishmael teased Sarah about being an old lady with a little boy. Sarah was so angry that she asked Abraham to send Hagar and Ishmael away. Abraham tried to calm Sarah down, but she would have none of it. It was a sensitive situation for Abraham … how do you chase your own son and his mother away? Abraham asked God for advice and I can just imagine that it sounded a little like this: "Oh Lord, what must I do? These women are driving me up the wall!"

The answer the Lord gave Abraham was not one he was expecting. He said that Sarah was right and that Hagar and Ishmael needed to go because Ishmael could not share in the inheritance with Isaac. In fact, God commanded Abraham to disinherit Ishmael (see Genesis 21).

What has this got to do with the Old Covenant and the New Testament? Paul explains it to the church in Galatia:

I would like to be present with you now and to change my tone; for I have doubts about you. Tell me, you who desire to be under the law, do you not hear the law? For it is written that Abraham had two sons: the one by a bondwoman, the other by a freewoman. But he who was of the bondwoman was born according to the flesh, and he of the freewoman through promise, which things are symbolic. For these are the two covenants: the one from Mount Sinai which gives birth to bondage, which is Hagar— for this Hagar is Mount Sinai in Arabia, and corresponds to Jerusalem which now is, and is in bondage with her children— but the Jerusalem above is free, which is the mother of us all. For it is written: "Rejoice, O barren, You who do not bear!

Break forth and shout, You who are not in labor! For the desolate has many more children than she who has a husband."

Now we, brethren, as Isaac was, are children of promise. But, as he who was born according to the flesh then persecuted him who was born according to the Spirit, even so it is now. Nevertheless what does the Scripture say? "Cast out the bondwoman and her son, for the son of the bondwoman shall not be heir with the son of the freewoman." So then, brethren, we are not children of the bond-woman but of the free.

Galatians 4:20-31

Ishmael was the son of a slave and Isaac the son of a "free" woman. The son of the slave was born as a result of Abraham's own efforts, while the son of the "free" woman was born as a result of God's promise (see Galatians 4:21).

Can you sense the tension? Abraham has two sons – one is the fruit of his own attempt and performance and the other is the fruit of the promise. His two wives represent the two covenants. Hagar, the concubine, represents the Old Covenant that was entered into on Mount Sinai and resulted in slavery. What happened on Mount Sinai? It was the mountain where Moses received the Ten Commandments. Hagar and Ishmael allude to the law and slavery. Hagar is also the image of Jerusalem today, and her inhabitants living in slavery (see Galatians 4:24-25).

Sarah, on the other hand, represents the New Testament. She brought a son into the world without working to accomplish it; he was given to her as a gift! She was not a slave and lived in total freedom:

*B*ut the other woman, Sarah, represents the heavenly Jerusalem. She is the free woman, and she is our mother. As Isaiah
said, "Rejoice, O childless woman, you who have never given birth!
Break into a joyful shout you who have never been in labour! For
the desolate woman now has more children than the woman who
lives with her husband!"

Galatians 4:26-27, NLT

Paul is comparing the earthly Jerusalem with the heavenly
Jerusalem. The earthly Jerusalem is tied to religion and
is in slavery along with her children. There are many
Christians who tend to go back to the customs of the Old
Covenant as if they will somehow bring deeper meaning
to their relationship with God. This is precisely what the
Galatians wanted to do when Paul rebuked them so fervently.

The spiritual Jerusalem – which is an image of the New
Testament church – lives in total freedom! The freedom
we received as a gift by grace is because we are in Christ!
Wouldn't you agree that the gospel of grace and our inheritance sometimes just sounds too good to be true? This
is the reason some believers keep feeling like they need to
add something...

The point is, you cannot balance grace with something
else. Grace is not a concept or a doctrine – it is a person,
Jesus Christ!

Because of Him we are children of the promise and beneficiaries of the New Testament!

Paul said this in so many words to the Galatians: "Chase the slave and her son away!" Ishmael and Isaac could not stay under one roof and could by no means share in the inheritance. Our inheritance is locked up in the grace of God and He does not want us to try to earn it. The gospel of grace loses its power when we mix it with our own efforts. Christ freed us so that we might be truly free. We need to stand firm in this freedom and not be forced under the yoke of slavery again!

Paul says that the smallest amount of yeast can sour the whole batch of dough (see Galatians 5:8b). He is clearly referring to religious traditions that stem from the Old Covenant. So many Christians want to grab hold of these traditions again, without knowing that these traditions are counter-productive to their maturity as Christians.

The prophetic references and practices in the Old Covenant were only a shadow of what would be fulfilled in the New Testament.

All the Jewish festivals – weekly, monthly and annually – were completely fulfilled in Christ. We cannot afford to hold onto Old Testament customs, due to our religious piety, in order to celebrate the reality of the New Testament. We mix the Old Covenant with the New Testament and render our faith powerless.

Along with the Law of Moses, we received rules, regulations and instructions. The focus was on external behaviour and whether it was right or wrong. It planted a performance - mentality in our psyche and awakened guilt and shame in us. It led to a life caught up in the cycle of guilt.

The new way asks for insight into the crucifixion of Jesus. This is to understand what He has done on our behalf. This understanding and realisation awakens us to grace and causes us to experience joy! Knowing that I am totally and utterly innocent before God draws me into an intimate relationship with Him!

9

CHRIST IS THE KEY

If there is one thing the average South African house has in common, it would be a safe. Even though it comes in many different shapes and sizes, it remains a safe place to store valuable items such as documents, weapons, jewellery and even spare keys. A safe is used to protect something of value against fire, theft and any other potential damage. There is also no way of accessing the items in the safe without the key.

In this book, we are in the process of opening up the wonderful gift of grace and discovering the extent of our inheritance in Christ. This chapter will focus on the key that opens up this gift – Jesus Christ. It is impossible to receive the grace of God and experience it in our lives without Him.

In Christ, God revealed His original plan for mankind. He is the centre of the Gospel and the One everything revolves around. In order to discover the grace of God, you need to discover Jesus Christ. If there is ever a conversation carried out about grace without honouring Christ, then the conversation is not really about grace – no matter how many times the word "grace" is used.

A new conversation

The writer of Hebrews begins the book with a striking statement, which he uses to lay the foundation for the thirteen chapters that follow:

God, who at various times and in various ways spoke in time past to the fathers by the prophets, has in these last days spoken to us by His Son...

Hebrews 1:1-2a

There are two different periods of time spoken about in this passage of Scripture. In the first period God spoke to man through prophets. God shared portions of His mystery with the prophets, like pieces of a puzzle. The prophets then had to communicate this message to the people. These prophecies were pointing to a new era or time period. There are various prophecies and events in the Old Testament that were all pointing to the saving work of Christ that would come.

For example, think of the time where Moses carefully explained to the Israelites that they needed to smear the blood of an innocent lamb on their door frames in order to spare the life of their eldest child. This was a clue of what would take place in the future. An eldest son would die one day and his blood would exempt us from death.

In the Old Testament there are many examples of how God spoke about the coming of His Son. God so clearly and consistently communicated this message that the Jews longed for the coming of the Messiah. Unfortunately, they did not recognise Him as the Messiah when He made His appearance.

In spite of their ignorance, that day finally dawned and it was no longer necessary to predict His coming. He became flesh and made His dwelling among us. He was crucified, was raised from the dead and the New Testament took effect.

It is no longer necessary for God to give us clues concerning Jesus through the prophets. That which God wanted to say through the prophets, He has already said and that which needed to take place, has already taken place.

The prophets represent a period of time that has already come to an end, which is why we cannot go to the Bible and think God will talk to us or work with us in the same way he did with Joseph or Noah. The way in which God worked with the people in that time period needs to be understood in the light of the new conversation He started through His Son. God chose to pronounce a new verdict over us in His Son. It is a new time period and God came and said something brand new to us. It is the dispensation of grace where we, out of His fullness, receive grace upon grace.

The grace of God is available to all people. As Christians, however, we have the ability to better hear and understand this grace than non-Christians, who are not tuned into it. As Christians, we need to be careful not to listen to this new conversation religiously. We can very easily miss it, just like the prodigal son's older brother, because we do not understand it.

This message of grace is locked up in the new conversation God began through His Son. This declaration God made over us has the capacity to radically change our lives. The Word of God has creative power in our lives. Words are spirit-vehicles – they make huge amounts of creative energy available. Our words are like seed that we sow, containing an inherent genetic code. When this seed falls on fertile ground, it has the potential to germinate, take root and bear fruit. Our words bring forth either life or death.

Today the airwaves are jam-packed with information in full colour. It remains invisible and inaudible, however, until we tune in a receiver to capture it on a specific frequency.

The Word of God is the same. We need to tune in our hearts to "receive" this declaration God made over us. Jesus often said to people: "Whoever has an ear to hear, let him hear." Obviously everyone had ears, but few actually tuned theirs in to hear the true message.

Our hearts are influenced by what we hear. It is interesting to see exactly how an ear is made to enable us to hear. In a series of complicated steps, air, bone and sound are employed to decipher sound – they work together intensely in the hearing process. It is an absolute wonder of creation that the ear is able to hear everything from the soft ticking of a small watch to the roar of a V6 engine.

There are a range of volume adjustments the ear is able to master and it has the ability to intensify sound up to almost a million times. The ear is an exceptional organ!

It is truly phenomenal that one of the most amazing organs in the body is used to hear the Word of God. However, in order to understand how we hear sound, we first need to understand sound. A sound is made through something that vibrates – like vocal chords or loudspeakers. These vibrations produce compressed pulses from air molecules bumping against other air molecules.

Just like a wave of water, a sound wave cannot simply stop and disappear when it reaches the instrument that will decipher or decode it, or when there is a barrier or obstruction in its path. The sound wave has one of three reactions in this case:

1. It bounces off the object or barrier

2. It deflects around the object or barrier

3. It forms part of the object itself

It is our choice whether or not the words God speaks will bounce off, deflect around or gain entrance to our hearts. When we read the Bible in the light of what God says about salvation, it becomes a brand new book in which Jesus says that His Word is spirit and life.

> *It is the Spirit who gives life; the flesh profits nothing. The words that I speak to you are spirit, and they are life.*
>
> **John 6:63**

God has always spoken to man. All His words, dreams and desires for mankind were gathered and accumulated together, and God spoke His heart out in Christ. God made a final declaration in order to be heard by all people. God could not have spoken to man more clearly than He did when He sent Christ to reveal His heart to us.

When we want to hear what God is saying to us we need to listen to what His Son is saying to us. What did God say to us then through His Son?

Two time periods, one book
The writer of Hebrews tries to make it clear that the New Testament is not just an extension of the Old Covenant, but rather a brand new conversation God has started about us:

> *But now He has obtained a more excellent ministry, inasmuch as He is also Mediator of a better covenant, which was estab-*

lished on better promises.

I think we get confused with the two different time periods presented in the Bible because they are incorporated into one book. The Old Covenant was simply telling us what would be coming in a new dispensation. The New Testament puts the Old Covenant in perspective for us. Somebody once said that the New is locked up in the Old and the Old is unlocked in the New – we only understand God's intentions in the Old Covenant in the light of the revelation of the New Testament.

Jesus is the key to eternal life

Jesus told his disciples just before He died that He was going to prepare a place for us and, once He had done so, that He would come back to take us there:

> "*Let not your heart be troubled; you believe in God, believe also in Me. In My Father's house are many mansions; if it were not so, I would have told you. I go to prepare a place for you. And if I go and prepare a place for you, I will come again and receive you to Myself; that where I am, there you may be also. And where I go you know, and the way you know." Thomas said to Him, "Lord, we do not know where You are going, and how can we know the*

way?" Jesus said to him, "I am the way, the truth, and the life. No one comes to the Father except through Me".

John 14:1-6

This was not, however, a reference to heaven, as most people think. It almost sounds like Jesus is in the middle of this extensive building project in heaven where teams of angels are busy mixing cement and carrying bricks in the hope the project will be completed in time. Once the project is finished, Jesus will come and fetch us and bring us to this "place" which, to many people, is a tangible place in heaven.

The fact is: Jesus does not need to build anything! Our God creates with a word! He does not have to spend two thousand years building a house!

What is this place that Jesus went to prepare for us and where He will take us when it is finished? Jesus is speaking here about the privilege of being welcome in the presence of the Father. Jesus went into the real Most Holy Place and sprinkled His own blood on the mercy seat so that our sins would be taken away for eternity. Jesus went to heaven and prepared the Most Holy Place – where man had been disqualified from entering for centuries. Jesus went to prepare a place for us in the presence of God. Jesus has already come to fetch us and has taken us to this place, which we see in Hebrews: "Come and approach the throne of grace with confidence!" (see Hebrews 4:26).

Doubting Thomas wanted to know where this place was where Jesus was going. Jesus then referred to Himself as the only key and entrance to the special place He had prepared for us. He is the way and the truth and the life. No-one comes to the Father except through Him (see John 14:6).

His DNA is in us – as He is, so are we on this earth. We grow in Him as we discover everything He has spoken over our lives.

Christ as the mirror image of my life

What do you see when you look in the mirror? This is not a trick question! Obviously you see yourself! A mirror is a very honest thing. It hides nothing and always tells the truth.

The Bible says that Christ is a mirror for us – when we look at Him He shows us what we look like now that we are in Him. Christ is the mirror in which we can see ourselves the way God sees us. Look at what this scripture says:

> *But we all, with unveiled face, beholding as in a mirror the glory of the Lord, are being transformed into the same image from glory to glory, just as by the Spirit of the Lord.*

> **2 Corinthians 3:18**

Paul says we see ourselves when we behold the glory of God. The Greek word for "glory" is *doxa*. When we *glorify* someone, we speak out kind and favorable words about that person.

In the Old Covenant, this word was primarily used to describe the weight of God's presence. Many times it went hand in hand with the visible or tangible presence of God.

Moses had a taste of this glory. In Exodus 34 we read how he spent forty days and forty nights on the mountain in the presence of God. This was also the time in which he received the Ten Commandments.

After forty days and nights Moses came down from the mountain ready to share everything God had told him with the people. His face shone so brightly from the glory, however, that the Israelites were afraid of him. But Moses knew that the radiant glory of God had begun to fade from his face, so he covered it with a veil so the Israelites would hopefully not notice.

This is what Paul was referring to when he told the Corinthians that we all need to behold the glory of God with unveiled faces. Moses represented the old dispensation where people only experienced moments of glory and were very aware how transient these were. Moses and the law remain a reminder of the Old Covenant and the law's inability to enable us to see the glory of God. This is why Paul says that when we read the law today, as if it is our reference for life, a veil covers us again and we simply become aware once again of our human shortcomings. But when we turn away from the law and look at the glory of our Saviour, we are invited into the freedom of His grace!

But even to this day, when Moses is read, a veil lies on their heart. Nevertheless when one turns to the Lord, the veil is taken away. Now the Lord is the Spirit; and where the Spirit of the Lord is, there is liberty.

2 Corinthians 3:15-17

When we become born again the covering that is over our hearts falls away. We are then able to easily see the glory of God and so discover our true identity! When Christ is the mirror in which we look at ourselves, we are able to see God's glory openly. In essence, glory means God's opinion or verdict – that which He has pronounced.

God made a new pronouncement over man when He sent His Son. We need to rediscover ourselves in Christ. Therefore, when we look at Christ the mirror, we see God's opinion about us and His Godly qualities that we share.

When we look into this mirror, our minds are changed and we begin to look more and more like who we really are. When we look at Christ, we don't just see the glory of God, but we see ourselves as God sees us. He came and duplicated in us the very qualities that we see and greatly admire in Him. The grain of wheat died and brought forth a great harvest.

No mirror shows you what you actually should look like or who you could be. A mirror only shows you what you look like now; it only shows you what a reality is currently. The more we look at ourselves in Christ, the more we begin to look like Him.

In his first letter, John says that as Jesus was in the world, so are we in this world (see 1 John 4:17). It makes so much more sense now that Jesus is not only an example for us, but that He is an example of us.

See yourself in Christ

We are thus transformed through seeing ourselves in Christ. In Christian counselling today, the popular approach is to focus on the person's past and history rather than focussing on his identity in Christ. It is as though we are trying to help each other accept our identity as sinners and then try to become better people through psychological practices. If you do not discover your true identity and know who you really are now that you are a new creation, you will continue to be weighed down under the power of guilt and shame and pain.

When we discover the glory of God, our likeness changes and we experience true freedom! The truth does not lie in unravelling your broken past, but in the revelation of your true identity in Christ.

The good news of the Gospel is that you are already who God originally created you to be! This was made possible through the work of grace in His Son, without you needing to do anything in your own strength!

Christ is the key to God's promises

Every promise God made us has been fulfilled in Christ. Paul says it doesn't matter how many promises God has given us, the answer is "yes" to each one!

The Message says it beautifully:

> Whatever God has promised gets stamped with the Yes of Jesus. In him, this is what we preach and pray, the great Amen, God's Yes and our Yes together, gloriously evident. God affirms us, making us a sure thing in Christ, putting his Yes within us. By his Spirit he has stamped us with his eternal pledge — a sure beginning of what he is destined to complete.
>
> *2 Corinthians 1:20-22*

Jesus is the culmination of every promise and prophecy of God's favor. Every possible reference of our lives gets redefined in the light of the revelation of Jesus Christ. Every expectation man has ever nurtured about himself throughout the ages has been made possible in Christ.

The awakening of faith

You don't have to attempt to become like Christ; all you need to do is look in the mirror and see that you already look like Him! This discovery results in your faith in God being awakened. Paul says that faith comes from hearing, and hearing from the Word of God. As you discover God's Word and allow it into your heart, your faith in Him begins to grow. God's faith is activated in you through the revelation of Christ and who you are in Him.

Everything God planned and destined for man He revealed to us in Christ:

- We died with Christ;

- We are buried with Him;

- We were raised together with Him;

- We are now seated with Him in heavenly places!

Jesus is the fulfilment of the redemption plan

Jesus came to tell us everything God had to say about man; He is the revelation of the new creation. It is when we look at Him that we are completely transformed in order to look like Him. This is why Paul warns us not to believe doctrines that are not the full truth:

> *Beware lest anyone cheat you through philosophy and empty deceit, according to the tradition of men, according to the basic principles of the world, and not according to Christ. For in Him dwells all the fullness of the Godhead bodily; and you are complete in Him, who is the head of all principality and power.*

> **Colossians 2:8-10**

Never allow failure or other people's opinions about you to cause you to believe you are not who God says you are!

You are the righteousness of God and you are empowered daily by His Spirit to discover yourself in Him!

10

FAVORED BY GOD

Everyone has a few favorites in life – from a specific chocolate, car or a cell phone brand to a particular TV programme. Most people will be able to tell you very convincingly why they prefer one thing over another.

Children are particularly prone to having a favorite toy. It reminds me of the little boy whose favorite toy was his soft, brown dog. The dog was eventually faded and washed out, but he still chose it above any of his other toys. This dog appeared in most of his photographs and it went with him everywhere – to church, to the shops and to bed. It wasn't the most expensive or the best looking of his toys, but this young owner had singled it out as his favorite. God does not favor us because we are so amazing – in some cases we pretty much represent the boy's drab dog. God, however, has attached distinct value to us.

In the Old Covenant there were specific people who experienced the favor of God on their lives.

We read about Joseph, his father's eleventh son. Jacob loved Joseph very much and showed his love for him by having a special colourful coat made for him. Jacob made no secret of the fact that this was his favorite child. And Joseph's brothers hated him because their father favored him.

On top of everything, Joseph shared his dreams with them which made them even more jealous. He dreamt that he and his brothers were gathering sheaves of wheat and that his brothers' sheaves bowed down before him. He also dreamt that even the sun, moon and stars bowed down before him.

God gave these dreams to Joseph, but because Joseph spoke about them too soon, his brothers decided to get rid of him and sell him as a slave. Joseph then found himself in a few difficult situations, but it was in these difficulties that the favor of God started to show in his life. He was successful in everything he did and he enjoyed great favor with his Egyptian master, Potiphar:

*A*nd his master saw that the Lord was with him and that the Lord made all he did to prosper in his hand. So Joseph found favor in his sight, and served him. Then he made him overseer of his house, and all that he had he put under his authority.

Genesis 39:3-4

Later on, after being wrongfully accused of misconduct and thrown in prison, God's favor continued to follow him. He wasn't in prison very long before the prison warder appointed him supervisor over the other prisoners.

After that, Joseph even interpreted one of the Pharaoh's dreams, and, in so doing, won his favor. After Joseph was released from prison, he became second in command of all Pharaoh's officials. With the wisdom God gave him, Joseph rescued Egypt from famine. And then, finally, without knowing who he was, his brothers came and bought wheat from him one day and bowed down before him.

Joseph's dream had come true! The dream was not only about Joseph, however, but the favor God gave him resulted in an entire nation being saved from famine!

Our second example is that of Ruth, a Moabite woman who also experienced the favor of God on her life. She married an Israelite who had moved to Moab with his parents, because of the great famine in the land of Israel. After her husband and two sons died (Ruth's husband being one of the two) Naomi, Ruth's mother-in- law, decided to return to the land of her birth. Ruth went with her, adopting Naomi's people and her God as her own.

One day, Ruth was busy collecting sheaves on Boaz's fields. Boaz was a member of her late father-in-law's family; was kind to her and showed her favor despite the fact that she was an unknown Moabite woman.

Boaz was a kinsman redeemer – a man with the responsibility of marrying a family-member's widow in order to ensure the deceased member's line would continue to the next generation. Ruth found favor in the eyes of Boaz and he married her. They were blessed with offspring and Jesus Christ was born from their bloodline! The favor Ruth experienced was again not just for her own benefit, but to give birth to descendants from whose lineage king David, and later Jesus Christ would be born, bringing salvation to all mankind.

A third person revealing God's favor was Esther. She was a young Jewish girl who went to live with her uncle Mordecai after the death of her parents. King Xerxes was looking for a new wife and he summoned the most beautiful girls from all the provinces to come to his palace. After a certain period of time, in which the girls received beauty treatments and followed a special diet, he would choose himself a wife from the group. Of all the beautiful women, it was Esther who drew the king's attention and found favor in his sight.

The king fell in love with her more than any of the other women and took her as his wife. Shortly after Esther became queen, she overheard that the king's top-ranked official, Haman, intended to wipe out all the Jews. Esther was her nation's only hope. "Yes, who knows whether you have become queen for such a time as this?" Mordecai said to her when they discussed this issue (see Esther 4:14).

It was against the law for anyone to approach the king without being summoned. Esther, however, decided to risk her life and go to ask the king to oppose Haman's proposal to have all the Jews killed. The Jews fasted and prayed for three days before Esther clothed herself in her royal attire and approached the king. Once again, Esther gained the favor of the king: he extended his golden sceptre to her as a sign of his favor.

Esther presented her case before the king and found favor with him. The king decreed that the Jews' lives would be spared and that Haman would be executed. The favor on Esther's life did not just make her queen, but also resulted in an entire nation being saved.

David, Daniel and Gideon were other examples of people in the Old Testament who enjoyed the favor of God in their generations and who experienced a taste of what we would experience in the new dispensation every day.

Christ ushers us into God's favor for our lives

Have you ever wished there could also be favor on your life? The Good News is that now that you are in Christ, God has already shown you grace and favor!

Just as the king extended his sceptre towards Esther as an indication of his favor toward her, God also extends His sceptre of favor towards us. We are now always welcome in His presence.

In Christ, we already live a life of grace and we no longer have to look forward to a certain time where we will one day experience His favor. The words "favor" and "grace" come from the same root word and mean to advantageously benefit others, to accept, to give preferential treatment and to find pleasure and delight in their company.

When you find favor with someone, you can go to them anytime and talk to them. To be favored by God means that we receive preferential treatment because He loves us – He takes pleasure in each one of us!

His heart's desire

Sometimes we may wonder how we gained God's grace and favor while we were still sinners. Just like Ruth, who wasn't even welcome amongst the Jews and yet found favor with Boaz, God showed us His grace without us deserving it.

God is rich in mercy and loves us so deeply that He paved a way for us to be with Him. He saved us by grace without any help or performance from our side.

Paul says in 2 Corinthians 5:29 that God reconciled the world to Himself in Christ and no longer holds their offenses against them.

The core message of the Gospel is that the relationship between God and man has been restored. Now, anyone who is in Christ is welcome in His presence. We never have to feel guilty or condemned in His presence ever again. Man is God's heart's dream...

*H*is association goes back to before the fall of the world, His love knew that He would present us again face to face before Him, identified in Christ in blameless innocence. He is the architect of our design; His heart dream realized our coming of age in Christ and to seal our sonship the spirit of His son echoes Abba Father in our hearts.

Ephesians 1:4-5, THE MIRROR

When God thinks about Jesus, He thinks about us; when He thinks about us, He sees us in His Son. God sees His beloved children in Christ and it provides Him endless joy.

God's work of art

In Ephesians 2:10 Paul uses the word *poiéma*, in the original language, the word from which the English word "poem" is derived. Some translations use the concept "handiwork" or "workmanship":

*F*or we are His workmanship, created in Christ Jesus for good works, which God prepared beforehand that we should walk in them.

Ephesians 2:10

We were created in Christ; each one of us is the unique work of His hands. God regards us as His property – He designed and devised us. We are the proud product of His own workmanship, His vision of love, His poetry!

The logic of God's love

Isn't it phenomenal to realise that God reached out to us while we were still far from Him? Why would God do this? What caused God to redeem us and reconcile us to Himself? What motivated Him to go as far as dying for us on a cross?

When God looks at us He sees companionship and love and this is what motivated Him. God placed value in man – He came and redeemed His own image and likeness in us. The death Christ died is the evidence of the price God was willing to pay to ransom mankind.

The preciousness of the blood of Jesus is directly linked to the worth of the item God purchased with it:

> ... knowing that you were not redeemed with corruptible things, like silver or gold, from your aimless conduct received by tradition from your fathers, but with the precious blood of Christ, as of a lamb without blemish and without spot.
>
> **1 Peter 1:18-19**

God sent Jesus to reveal man's inherent worth. Man's identity is intertwined with God's opinion of him.

Dust is not your origin, nor is it your fate. There is a greater reality about who you are, which is what motivated Him to pay the price. When you begin to understand the love of God, you cannot help responding in love, because love generates love!

*B*ut God demonstrates His own love toward us, in that while we were still sinners, Christ died for us. Much more then, having now been justified by His blood, we shall be saved from wrath through Him. For if when we were enemies we were reconciled to God through the death of His Son, much more, having been reconciled, we shall be saved by His life. And not only that, but we also rejoice in God through our Lord Jesus Christ, through whom we have now received the reconciliation.

Romans 5:8-11

Jesus Christ is the standard of God's grace and love

God saw the end product of His love offering in Christ's suffering, and it pleased Him. The significance of Jesus' death and resurrection is what gives the Gospel its impact:

*H*e shall see the labour of His soul, and be satisfied. By His knowledge My righteous Servant shall justify many, for He shall bear their iniquities.

Isaiah 53:11

THE MESSAGE version of Isaiah 53:11 is striking in its description:

Out of that terrible travail of soul, he'll see that it's worth it and be glad he did it. Through what he experienced, my righteous one, my servant, will make many "righteous ones", as he himself carries the burden of their sins.

The fact that God calls man into a relationship is evidence of His eternal love for us. Our innocence, bought with the blood of Jesus, makes it possible for us to have a relationship with Him. The same innocence that characterised the life of Jesus is now also ours.

For years, man's framework was darkness. John confirmed that the people living in darkness saw a great light (see John 1:9). They became part of this light after believing for years they were just dust and sinners. They realised who they really were; they realised they had been created in the image and likeness of God!

The eternal echo
There is an eternal echo in the heart of every person – God created everyone with the sole purpose of living in an intimate relationship with Him. Golgotha was the motive to see this need realised. The worth He attached to man explains the tremendously high price He paid for our redemption: the precious blood of His Son.

His plan was to lift us out of the dust of our sinner's mentality and to introduce us to our true, Godly identity. He carried this desire in His heart for centuries – this desire to reconcile us to Himself so we could be His prized possession.

This is why the prophet Zephaniah cries out in chapter 3:17: "The Lord your God in your midst, the Mighty One, will save; He will rejoice over you with gladness, He will quiet you with His love, He will rejoice over you with singing." Our true identity cannot be measured by time, status, origin or gender. Man is the bearer of God's image, likeness and glory!

Every person – regardless of race or background – has equal value, which is why we cannot, under any circumstances, continue to judge people according to external factors. Paul says we no longer know people according to the flesh because, even though we once knew Christ in the flesh, we no longer know Him in this way (see 2 Corinthians 5:16).

In Christ, we are all equal before God and we, therefore, have no right to deem anyone less worthy. We all have the same Lord and He is Lord of all and richly blesses everyone who calls on Him.

For there is no distinction between Jew and Greek, for the same Lord over all is rich to all who call upon Him.

Romans 10:12

Bearers of His glory

God does not consider man to be an inferior spirit-associate. Christ came and showed us that the glory of God could take form in a physical body, which is why our bodies are worthy carriers of the glory of God.

Jesus did not come to start a new religion. He also did not come to begin Christianity. People tend to turn the Good News into a religion. Jesus came to reconcile man to God and to introduce man to his true self! Jesus came to show man how God originally created him: innocent, justified and a bearer of His glory.

While we were still His enemies, God reconciled us by the blood of His Son. How much more will we not be saved through His life, now that we have been reconciled?

God took the initiative

God took the first step to restore our relationship between Himself and man. He took the initiative and first proved His love for us. We now have the choice whether to love Him back or not. God is the source of love – not man. When His love is in me, it flows back to Him and to the people around me. This means that I can love effortlessly, without even trying. His love in us awakens our love for Him and for others.

Grace restores intimacy between God and man

God created each of us as a unique work of art with the sole purpose of experiencing His favor and grace so that we can be bearers of His glory. God's grace reconciled us to Himself and it had two primary consequences. Firstly, it restored intimacy between ourselves and God and secondly, it restored our power and authority as rulers.

As a result of our intimacy with God being restored, we are free from the guilt and shame which enslaved our lives. Guilt and shame are the products of sin which robbed us of intimacy with God. The reality is: if you feel guilty and ashamed you will never feel free or confident to be in His presence.

Christ's proclamation – "it is finished" is the receipt, the proof of payment, verifying that our debt with God has been paid off. We are eternally exempt from our debt because Someone else paid it on our behalf. There is, therefore, no longer any reason why we cannot enter His presence freely and confidently. We owe Him nothing – the debt has been settled for us! This is what it means to be acquitted or justified!

God wants to overwhelm us with his grace

What is the implication of our redemption? It means there is no further condemnation for us. Christ does not feel guilty in the Father's presence, because He did nothing about which to feel guilty. The same applies to you – you have nothing to feel guilty about because Jesus accomplished full redemption on your behalf.

There is therefore now no condemnation to those who are in Christ Jesus, who do not walk according to the flesh, but according to the Spirit.

Romans 8:1

In chapter 8, Paul continues to describe how God has given us everything – that He did not even spare His own Son, but that He did everything and gave everything – in order to have a love relationship with us once again.

To confirm our innocence, Paul asks the following question: "Who dares accuse us whom God has chosen for his own? No one – for God himself has given us right-standing with himself." (Romans 8:33a, NLT).

Every accusation against man has been cancelled. God invites us into a relationship without borders, unimpeded, unlimited and unbroken. Nothing could ever happen to undo this relationship ever again – nothing man could ever do could separate him from the love of God.

Grace in action

When you discover this truth and realise who you really are, you begin to live differently. You are now innocent because you are the righteousness of God – it unlocks the grace of God and makes it visible in your life.

Can you imagine what the impact would be if you discovered the grace of God and the full truth about your identity? Could this not be the very reason why you are alive at such a time as this – the reason you find yourself in your city, amongst the people you interact with every day?

You are God's favorite! May the grace of God touch the lives of many people through you!

11
ENTER THE REST

Let us reflect on the essence of the Gospel. So often, it is presented as a framework of Christian values and certain things we have to do in order to qualify for the favor of God. Our reward for our devotion has always been presented as heaven. We are, however, no longer in the process of playing spiritual "Snakes and Ladders".

We have discovered that the Gospel is so much more than an attempt to qualify for the privilege of going to live in a beautiful place one day. Naturally, heaven implies the privilege of enjoying the continuous and uninterrupted pleasure of God's glory – and every believer looks forward to this. But there is so much more to the Gospel, because the good news is that we can already partake in the glory of God.

The concept of the Gospel means good news. And for good news to be good news, it really must be good news!

The foundational Scripture we looked at to explain the good news was Romans 5:17:

*F*or if by the one man's offense death reigned through the one,
much more those who receive abundance of grace and of the
gift of righteousness will reign in life through the One, Jesus Christ.

You are welcome to go and study the "much more" references in the letter to the Romans but you will discover that
"much more" really does mean just that – "**much more**"!

Adam experienced a certain quality of life before sin got
a hold on him. His sin caused man's quality of life to drop
to a lower level – a life of inferiority and limitation. Yet,
"much more" took place! What does this life of "much more"
mean? It means that Adam is no longer my frame of reference for how I should live. Adam is no longer the standard
against which I measure myself. My life is measured against
a new standard: Christ Jesus. Christ is now the definition
of my true identity – of who I am. In Romans 8, Paul says:

*F*or whom He foreknew, He also predestined to be conformed
to the image of His Son, that He might be the firstborn among
many brethren.

Romans 8:29

The Bible is not about understanding and trying to pursue
certain guidelines to attempt to better myself. It is not a
showcase of something I have to try to obtain. The Bible
is a mirror that reveals to me who I already am. The Bible

reveals God's complete verdict spoken over us, as revealed in His Son, Jesus Christ.

The word-mirror is the key to understanding the whole Bible

When you discover yourself in the full glory and full identity of Christ, you begin to experience the glory of God over your life and abundant life becomes a reality for you.

The confirmation of your true identity lies within this understanding. This new identity is the foundation of your core being. If you think differently about who you are, you will think differently about how you live.

Identity determines behaviour

This principle is spelled out for us so clearly in the account of the twelve spies of Israel. They had to go and spy out the land of Canaan and deliver a report on how Israel should take possession of this Promised Land. God had already appointed this land as their inheritance and they now needed to respond in faith to take possession of it. However, they forfeited this inheritance for an entire generation because their opinion of themselves was extremely negative. They saw themselves as grasshoppers in comparison to the inhabitants of the Promised Land. The fact that they saw themselves in this way determined their behaviour!

*B*ut the men who had gone up with him said, "We are not able to go up against the people, for they are stronger than we." And they gave the children of Israel a bad report of the land which they had spied out, saying, "The land through which we have gone as spies is a land that devours its inhabitants, and all the people whom we saw in it are men of great stature. There we saw the giants (the descendants of Anak came from the giants); and we were like grasshoppers in our own sight, and so we were in their sight."

Numbers 13:31-33

It is this typical inferiority complex that continues to keep believers away from the fullness of the "Promised Land" experience of the New Testament. The writer of Hebrews refers to this as God's rest. The Promised Land was a place of abundance and rest for Israel and it was a shadow of the reality of the New Testament. Our new life in Christ is a life of abundance and rest for every believer. We must not, however, live in the same disobedience or lack of faith, and in this way miss out on what God has already established for us.

*A*nd to whom did He swear that they would not enter His rest, but to those who did not obey? So we see that they could not enter in because of unbelief.

Hebrews 3:18-19

God honours Caleb, one of the spies who did not allow himself to be intimidated by the giants. He tried to convince the people that what God had promised them should not be influenced by their natural senses. He encouraged them to go and possess the land as their inheritance.

Then Caleb quieted the people before Moses, and said, "Let us go up at once and take possession, for we are well able to overcome it."

Numbers 13:30

The people, however, chose not to do so and paid the price by spending forty years in the desert – an entire generation. God rewarded the dedication of Joshua and Caleb, however, and of all twelve spies they were the only ones who later had the privilege of entering the Promised Land. The Lord gave Caleb a promise:

But My servant Caleb, because he has a different spirit in him and has followed Me fully, I will bring into the land where he went, and his descendants shall inherit it.

Numbers 14:24

Enter the Rest

We enter into this rest, or Promised Land, when we accept the word or verdict God has spoken over our lives in faith!

This word is what God came and said to us in His Son, Jesus Christ. It is in Christ that we discover our full inheritance – He is the origin of all reality.

In the beginning was the Word, and the Word was with God, and the Word was God. He was in the beginning with God. All things were made through Him, and without Him nothing was made that was made.

John 1:1-3

The Word produced everything. Christ, the Word, became flesh and made His dwelling among us and we beheld His glory and received grace upon grace out of His fullness.

God sent His eternal Word into this world so that we could come alive to His original created purpose for our lives – to our original design. God made us alive to this life in His Son. We place our trust in God's verdict that gives us access to His rest, which He intended for us.

For if Joshua had given them rest, then He would not afterward have spoken of another day. There remains therefore a rest for the people of God. For he who has entered His rest has himself also ceased from his works as God did from His. Let us therefore be diligent to enter that rest, lest anyone fall according to the same example of disobedience. For the word of God is living and powerful, and sharper than any two-edged sword, piercing even to the divi-

sion of soul and spirit, and of joints and marrow, and is a discerner
of the thoughts and intents of the heart.

Hebrews 4:8-12

This is why Scripture tells us we can enter this rest, because there remains a rest for God's people. Just like the Israelites needed to grab hold of the Word and believe it, it remains the foundation of experiencing this rest today. How do we enter this rest? By discovering and believing the finished reality of the Word.

As God rests, so do we

For he who has entered His rest has himself also ceased from his works as God did from His. Let us therefore be diligent to enter that rest...

Hebrews 4:10-11a

Like God, we can also enter a Sabbath rest. The first question is naturally: How does God rest?

The concept of rest refers back to what happened in the account of creation in Genesis. Scripture tells us that God created everything in six clear dispensations, or days. God "worked hard" for six days by creating everything, including man and woman.

And on the seventh day God rested (see Genesis 2:3). This was certainly not because He was tired from the previous six days of hard work. God cannot get tired – He is the source of eternal energy!

Have you not known? Have you not heard? The everlasting God, the Lord, The Creator of the ends of the earth, Neither faints nor is weary. His understanding is unsearchable.

Isaiah 40:28

Behold, He who keeps Israel shall neither slumber nor sleep.

Psalm 121:4

What does this rest, into which God entered and which we have been invited to experience, mean for us?

I believe the key lies in Hebrews 4:12a:

For the word of God is living and powerful, and sharper than any two-edged sword...

God created with His word. He simply said, "Let there be light," and there was light. He sent His word with the absolute conviction that it would accomplish the purpose for which it was sent.

The Bible tells us in Hebrews 1:3 that God holds everything together by the word of His power. God's Word is His power. The Amplified Bible puts it like this:

He is maintaining and propelling and guiding the universe by his mighty word of power.

Hebrews 1:3

It is not the power of His word; it is the word of His power. There is a substantial difference. Let me use the following example to explain: If I tell you I'm going to hit you with the power of my arm, I am then referring to the power that is locked up in my arm. But if I tell you I'm going to hit you with the arm of my power, I am then saying that my arm represents and facilitates the focused release of my full power and my full ability.

Therefore, when the Bible says that God holds everything together by the word of His power, it means the Word of God represents His full power. We know this Word was with God, and the Word was God, and all things were made through Him, and without Him nothing was made that has been made. And we beheld His glory and we discovered that Christ was the Word of God.

As we discover Christ we discover God's Word, which is His creative declaration or verdict over our lives. Within this insight and revelation we enter into God's rest with the absolute conviction that God's Word will accomplish the purpose for which He sent it in our lives!

Hebrews 4 goes on to say:

*F*or the word of God is living and powerful, and sharper than any two-edged sword, piercing even to the division of soul and spirit, and of joints and marrow, and is a discerner of the thoughts and intents of the heart.

Hebrews 4:12

The Word of God is living and active, it brings division between soul and spirit and judges the heart. When we get the revelation that we are included in His inheritance, it causes a division between the realm of our soul and the realm of our spirit. The Word brings about the division between the limited realm of the soul and the unlimited dimension of the spirit, the environment from which we are now enabled to live.

The Word of God is living and active, enabling me to discern or distinguish between soul-based references and spiritual reality. When we get the revelation that we are included in His inheritance, it causes a 'separation' between the realm of our soul and the realm of our spirit, empowering me to step away from the limited realm of the soul into the unlimited dimension of the spirit. It launches me out of the limited reference of the soul's demands – the thoughts and intents of the heart – into the uninhibited environment of life in Christ as God intended.

We enter God's rest by discovering and believing the finished reality of the Word. In Him we live, and move and have our being!

As God rests, so we can rest

The people could not enter this rest because they did not believe. I, however, am able to enter into this inheritance through faith in the finished work of Christ.

When Jesus was tempted in the desert He resisted the temptation by saying: "it is written" (see Luke 4:4,8,10). The book of Luke uses the Greek word *logos* here. On the fourth time, however, Jesus' counter statement is translated as: "it is said" (see Luke 4:12). This is the Greek word *rhema*. Although we are careful not to add our own interpretations to the word, *logos* indicates more the general, written word of God and *rhema* indicates the revealed word – when the word becomes alive to us. It would seem that Jesus – the *Logos* – continues to identify Himself fully with God's original verdict until it gained a foothold in His spirit and He could speak out a *rhema* word (a fresh, Spirit-inspired revelation word). The Bible says the enemy then left Him.

We place our trust in Christ and we confidently declare His word over our circumstances. We are no longer intimidated by what our senses tell us, because we have experienced how the Word brings division and distinction in our lives as we now live by the Spirit.

Christ has done everything on our behalf so that we can live a life of victory. He meant it when He cried out: "It is finished!"

We have been destined to live in this framework of "it is finished" for all eternity and our desire is for every person to make this discovery! This is the message of good news for every person on this planet!

It's not Do but Done!

ALAN PLATT
LEADER AND FOUNDER OF DOXA DEO

Alan Platt is an agent of transformation in the lives of individuals, local churches and corporate structures of society. He has been in full-time ministry since 1983, serving the church on various levels. Under his leadership of Doxa Deo, a strong city-reaching strategy has been established. In Tshwane (Pretoria, South Africa) Doxa Deo serves 30,000 people (referred to as partners) in ten different campuses (local churches functioning as one integrated church in the city).

This Ministry has also established churches in five other cities in South-Africa, as well as three internationally (London, UK: Auckland, NZ; and Stuttgart, DE).

Doxa Deo has established various educational institutions (Pre, Elementary, through to High Schools) that serve to educate the next generation in Christ Centred education. Intentional engaging of existing public educational institutions by having a permanent presence in State schools in South Africa is part of their ministry strategy to affect the transformation of communities.

Vocational Education and Training Centres have been established to prepare people vocationally, also reaching the students spiritually, emotionally and physically through a counselling, medical, dental and eye care services.

The Ministry reaches out to HIV, abandoned and Special Needs children in several orphanages managed by The Doxa Deo Ministry.

Through their City Changers Institute, people are trained for effectiveness vocationally in the areas of Church, Education, Social Society and Business.

The City Changers movement has been birthed by the Doxa Deo ministry to facilitate greater integration and synergy between the kingdom initiatives in the different spheres of society.

Through Alan's primary gifting in leadership and teaching, he has not only established an exceptionally dynamic leadership team in Doxa Deo, but he has also influenced a wide spectrum of organisations, denominations and church networks internationally. His influence extends beyond the church to the influencing of the business sector, education and society at large.

Alan's capacity to communicate with small groups as well as large crowds makes him a sought-after speaker across the globe. His material on the finished work of Christ, as well as the Church and City Transformation has impacted many people, leaders and ministries. Alan has recently authored his second book titled 'City Changers', fast becoming a life changing instrument for many ministries.

Alan is married to Leana and they have two married children, Duncan and Amy.

Find more of Alan's thoughts at alanplatt.org.